A Bucket of Water

To: Miriam Amaka Odenigbo
       Ujunwa

With compliments and best wishes from the author, Kanayo F. Nwanze

Montreal, 28 Sep 2017

Praise for this book

'This book is an inspirational call to action by one of Africa's leading development champions.'
*Professor Calestous Juma, Harvard Kennedy School,
Cambridge, United States*

'This book has inspired me and given me fresh ideas. It feeds the will and the mind. A "must read", particularly for young men and women entering the field of rural development.'
*Julio Berdequé, Principal Researcher at the Latin-American Centre
for Rural Development (RIMISP), Santiago, Chile*

'This book is about the hard work of providing justice for individuals and communities. It could not be stronger on the cost of inaction – especially in Africa. The author's experience and passion for working with rural communities shines through from these pages.'
*Agnes M. Kalibata, President,
The Alliance for a Green Revolution in Africa (AGRA)*

'The book is a clear testimony of Dr Nwanze's dedication, commitment and passion to bring development to benefit smallholder farmers, women, and food insecure. It will inspire many who are working in agriculture and rural development in their pursuit of ending hunger and malnutrition.'
*Shenggen Fan, Director General,
International Food Policy Research Institute*

'A book of hope for the poorest people on the planet. In an engaging, uplifting, readable and lucid way, Kanayo Nwanze tackles the highly complex issue of rural transformation by taking the reader through dozens of practical examples of lives improved. His stories of international cooperation to strengthen opportunity and dignity for struggling people should overcome cynics everywhere. Why shouldn't we live in world free of hunger? Nwanze shows it can be done.'

Homi Kharas, Senior Fellow and Deputy Director, Global Economy and Development, The Brookings Institution, Washington D.C.

'Poverty and hunger are at the top of the world development agenda, encapsulated in the SDGs. Both are strongly linked to rural areas and farming. Smallholder farmers are key here – they must move from subsistence farming to profitable business, not only for their well-being but for our own food security. Kanayo Nwanze writes with authority and great understanding but also with passion. This is an important plea by Nwanze for all of us to focus on what really matters.'

Mo Ibrahim, Founder and Chairman, Mo Ibrahim Foundation

'An illuminating look at the challenges smallholder farmers face, but also the opportunities. Kanayo brings both academic rigour and a visionary, practitioner's view of what it will take to achieve an end to hunger.'

Winnie Byanyima, Executive Director, Oxfam International

A Bucket of Water

Reflections on Sustainable Rural Development

Kanayo F. Nwanze

PRACTICAL ACTION
Publishing

Practical Action Publishing Ltd
The Schumacher Centre, Bourton on Dunsmore, Rugby, Warwickshire, CV23 9QZ, UK
www.practicalactionpublishing.org

© International Fund for Agricultural Development (IFAD), 2017

The moral right of the author to be identified as author of the work has been asserted under sections 77 and 78 of the Copyright Designs and Patents Act 1988.

All rights reserved. No part of this publication may be reprinted or reproduced or utilized in any form or by any electronic, mechanical, or other means, now known or hereafter invented, including photocopying and recording, or in any information storage or retrieval system, without the written permission of the publishers.

Product or corporate names may be trademarks or registered trademarks, and are used only for identification and explanation without intent to infringe.

A catalogue record for this book is available from the British Library.

A catalogue record for this book has been requested from the Library of Congress.

ISBN 9781853399701 Hardback
ISBN 9781853399718 Paperback
ISBN 97817804499715 eBook
ISBN 9781780449708 Library PDF

Citation: Nwanze, K.F., *A Bucket of Water: Reflections on Sustainable Rural Development*, Rugby, UK: Practical Action Publishing and IFAD
<http://dx.doi.org/10.3362/97817804499708>.

Since 1974, Practical Action Publishing has published and disseminated books and information in support of international development work throughout the world. Practical Action Publishing is a trading name of Practical Action Publishing Ltd (Company Reg. No. 1159018), the wholly owned publishing company of Practical Action. Practical Action Publishing trades only in support of its parent charity objectives and any profits are covenanted back to Practical Action
(Charity Reg. No. 247257, Group VAT Registration No. 880 9924 76).

The views and opinions in this publication are those of the author and do not represent those of Practical Action Publishing Ltd or its parent charity Practical Action or IFAD. Reasonable efforts have been made to publish reliable data and information, but the authors and publisher cannot assume responsibility for the validity of all materials or for the consequences of their use.

The designations employed and the presentation of material in this publication do not imply the expression of any opinion whatsoever on the part of IFAD concerning the legal status of any country, territory, city or area or of its authorities, or concerning the delimitation of its frontiers or boundaries. The designations 'developed' and 'developing' countries are intended for statistical convenience and do not necessarily express a judgement about the stage reached in the development process by a particular country or area.

Cover photo: Women collect water in the Koulikoro region of southern Mali.
©Amadou Keita
Cover design by Andrew Corbett
Typeset by vPrompt eServices, India
Printed in the United Kingdom

Dedication

*During my long involvement in agricultural development,
I have been impressed again and again by the tireless contribution
that rural women make to their families, their communities,
and their countries. Often unacknowledged, disadvantaged, and
discriminated against in many ways, rural women are the heart and
soul of their communities. Without them there would be no food
security and no future. This book is dedicated to them.*

Contents

About the author	x
Foreword	xi
Preface	xv
Acknowledgements	xix
1. Dignity for all	1
2. Sowing conflict or growing peace?	13
3. Farming as a business	25
4. Where are the farmers of tomorrow?	45
5. Moving closer to gender equality	63
6. Climate change: the time is now	79
7. Development starts at home	95
8. Science, technology, and innovation	115
9. The cost of inaction	131
10. The future of farming	147
References	165

About the author

Kanayo F. Nwanze is President of the International Fund for Agricultural Development (IFAD), a specialized agency of the United Nations and an international financial institution. Previously, he was Director-General for a decade of what is now the Africa Rice Center, part of the Consultative Group on International Agricultural Research (CGIAR). He has been a member of the World Economic Forum's Global Agenda Council on Food Security since 2010. In 2016 he received the inaugural Africa Food Prize in recognition of his leadership of IFAD and advocacy for smallholder farmers.

Foreword

Kanayo Nwanze and I have been colleagues and friends for many years. I first got to know him in 1998 when I was president of the Rockefeller Foundation and he was director-general of West African Rice Development Association (WARDA), now the Africa Rice Center (AfricaRice) of the Consultative Group on International Agricultural Research (CGIAR). The Foundation helped to fund AfricaRice's path-breaking development of New Rice for Africa (NERICA), which Nwanze oversaw.

We soon discovered that we were both trained as entomologists; we had seen at first hand the terrible depredations of insects that attack the crops of poor farmers. We also both recognized that solving such problems is rarely easy and requires clear analysis, good science, and the placing of smallholder farmers at the centre of the solutions.

Nwanze has been on an exciting journey since then. For the past eight years he has led the International Fund for Agricultural Development (IFAD) in a determined and successful attempt to find practical and effective ways of tackling poverty in the rural areas of the developing world, where three-quarters of the poorest people live. He and I agree that the pathways towards the goal of poverty eradication must be open to all and built to last, or, to use the buzzwords of today, both inclusive and sustainable. And as scientists we demand that empirical evidence should be the bedrock on which these pathways are built.

Nwanze shares his most heartfelt beliefs in the chapters that follow. He champions the idea that inclusive rural development must begin with people – with women, men and youth, their families, and their communities. As a scientist, Nwanze is also convinced of the power of research and technology to improve lives – but only if handled wisely and coupled with an understanding of context and people's participation.

IFAD is the only United Nations agency to focus solely on rural areas. And Nwanze is a persistent advocate for increased investment in those areas, where hunger and poverty are concentrated, yet where small farms account for most food production. As he likes to point out 'crops don't grow by themselves'. Farmers need investment and technical and business skills. They also need to be able to underpin their efforts with inputs, finance, and insurance.

During his tenure as president of IFAD, Nwanze has received many accolades for his outstanding contributions to rural development. He was recently awarded the first Africa Food Prize in recognition of his unstinting support for agricultural development on his home continent.

Accepting the Africa Food Prize, Nwanze said, 'I would like to dedicate this award to the millions of African women who silently toil to feed their families. No nation has been able to transform itself without giving women the same rights and opportunities as men. Our hope for future generations rests with African women who bear and raise our young people who will shape the African continent in the years to come.'

Nwanze can also be justifiably outspoken. He has not been afraid to speak out against corruption and to call upon national leaders, particularly in Africa, to live up to their promises and honour their many commitments. Sometimes Nwanze's words may seem harsh and pessimistic. When he accepted the Africa Food Prize he asked the question: 'Can we say there has been progress when a region as rich as Africa is unable to feed itself?'

But Nwanze is also an optimist – and I share his optimism. As chief spokesperson of IFAD, he has been a passionate advocate on behalf of smallholder farmers and poor producers. He has campaigned tirelessly for their key role to be recognized, prioritized, and invested in; and his dedication and optimism have been rewarded. Agenda 2030 – the new global vision for sustainable development – has a target specifically for small-scale food producers: to double their productivity and their incomes by 2030.

In the hundreds of speeches, statements, and interviews made as president of IFAD, Nwanze has repeated what I have come to think of as his mantra: 'farming is a business'. And today it has become part of mainstream development discourse.

A Bucket of Water is an invaluable contribution to international dialogue and debate on rural issues. It underlines the key message – also confirmed by IFAD's *Rural Development Report 2016* – that inclusive rural transformation does not happen automatically as a result of broader economic growth. It must be made to happen if the rural areas – and the poorest sectors of society that call them home – are to share in the benefits of structural transformation and increased prosperity.

The book draws on Nwanze's experiences as a leader, but it also returns repeatedly to the rural communities he has visited, where IFAD and its partners work. It's a compendium of lessons learned by someone with a gift not just for speaking, but for listening too. Nwanze has listened hard to the many rural women and men he has met during his travels, and they are the book's main protagonists. We learn, for example, of life in the remote state of Jharkland in India, where moneylenders and extremist groups were adding to the miseries of poverty for tribal groups until an IFAD-funded project started working with the community. From Egypt, we hear the story of farmers who are now growing fresh fruit and vegetables on reclaimed desert land. We meet Zoeliharimalala Nirinarisoa in Madagascar, who makes yogurt with *moringa* to sell at the market.

Their stories speak of courage and they give hope. And with the household methodologies pioneered by IFAD and partners to strengthen gender equality, we see that poor families are willing and able to embrace change, perhaps more so than leaders, and step into a new future.

Nwanze believes that hunger and poverty can be consigned to the history books within the next generation. We have both been very lucky to have lived long and fulfilling professional lives and we wish the same for those that come after us – for the young people of today. Nwanze is a passionate advocate on behalf of young women and men. And once again, his commitment and determination have helped put the issue of youth and agriculture on the international agenda. This book reminds us that agriculture needs young people, and young people need agriculture, because urban sectors will not provide jobs for all the young people entering the labour markets in the coming decades.

Nwanze leads a unique people-centred organization that focuses on building people's capacity to make change happen. *A Bucket of Water* is also unique because it is a personal, heartfelt book, rich in humanity. It deserves to be widely read and shared.

Sir Gordon Conway
Chair of International Development at Imperial College, London,
and former President of the Rockefeller Foundation

Preface

Where I come from in Nigeria, there is a saying that when you go to the stream to fetch water, your bucket will only be filled with the water that is yours. No one can take the water that is meant for you. Life will give you what you deserve, nothing more, and nothing less. But first you must walk to the stream, bend down, and dip your bucket.

This is a parable about destiny. It may seem strange as a title for a book on development, which is all about possibility, opportunity, theories of change, transformation. And above all, it is about choices, and making the future better than the present.

But there is a connection – just as there is a connection between all of us, though we are individuals.

The sustainable development agenda that was agreed by world leaders in 2015, known as the 2030 Agenda, is universal. In setting out a goal of ending hunger and poverty, it vows to 'leave no one behind'. It is a collective decision taken by world leaders after a long and intensive process of deliberation and consensus building, in order to secure a sustainable future for humanity and this planet we share with all living things.

It was, significantly, a decision about our *collective* destiny. No one gets their bucket of water if there is no longer any river. The 2030 Agenda addresses the conditions and environment we need to create for each person to live with dignity and achieve their fullest potential.

As a scientist, and as the head of a fund that is both a United Nations agency and an international financial institution, I know that vision and commitment are important, but there also have to be resources to back them up.

Development has a price. But so does lack of development. There is a cost to inaction. We see it every day in poor and hungry people, fleeing populations, withered fields, volatile prices, crumbling infrastructure, stifled trade, options foreclosed or never offered, luxury amid poverty, instability and inequality. This is the cost of inaction. Some countries remain at the bottom of the development ladder, and hunger and poverty still stalk neglected areas – mainly rural – of nations that have graduated to middle-income status.

Things could be otherwise. IFAD has a long history of going to some of the remotest and resource-poor areas of the world and delivering innovative programmes that change people's lives and get development moving. And no matter how deprived the context, there is always the vast potential of the people themselves. In my previous career as a scientist, I saw first-hand how research directed at solving the problems of poor and marginalized people could produce solutions that saved lives – because we were focused, because we worked in the field with people, and because we believed that they mattered.

I am proud that IFAD is known as an honest broker, trusted by governments and by farmers alike. Within the UN family, we are a unique partner, connecting all the players in the agricultural and rural sectors so that everyone benefits. At a time when many donors are shifting to bilateral approaches, IFAD remains a model of multilateral cooperation. We are constantly testing innovative approaches, whether based on the latest technology or adapted from traditional knowledge. We scale up our successes to achieve greater impact, and gladly share results with our partners.

Achieving the 2030 Agenda will require innovation. The price tag is in the billions, if not trillions. Who should pay that price? Donors and development agencies? National governments? The private sector? To ask the question in that way would be to fundamentally misunderstand the crossroads in history where we are. If you look at development and ask 'What's in it for me?', the answer is, everything. The world today faces urgent challenges – conflict, migration and forced displacement, climate change, militancy, terrorism, environmental degradation – that threaten development gains made in recent decades and undermine prospects for global stability in the years ahead. They affect everyone, and must be faced together. The 17 Sustainable Development Goals (SDGs) are not a menu, but lenses through which we can see the interlocking and overlapping issues that affect us all – and indeed, that bind us together.

The 2030 Agenda is universal, which some might think makes it idealistic or utopian. I consider it realistic because it addresses problems that will not wait. There is no more practical goal than survival, and our survival is an indivisible whole. But I emphasize again that it is a collective goal. We must all reach the stream on our own to fill our bucket: the river will not come to us. But some struggle to reach the river more than others. So when we have fetched our bucket of water, we must share it with others less fortunate, because our future is interconnected.

During my tenure as president of IFAD (2009–17), I travelled extensively to capital cities and rural areas, delivered speeches and statements at conferences and meetings, lectures and seminars at universities. But most fulfilling of all, I visited field projects and programmes financed by IFAD and I interacted with rural communities. In the following chapters, I have tried to capture my experiences and stories from the field, discussions with presidents, prime ministers, ministers, project staff, and rural people. I look at the challenges of development – particularly in rural areas, where most of the poorest and hungry people live – as challenges for the world, for countries, for communities, for institutions, and above all for individuals. But amidst these challenges, I see huge opportunities with tremendous dividends. By investing in people we can change the world.

Acknowledgements

This book would not have been possible without the contributions of many people. As president of IFAD, I have travelled across the world to visit IFAD-supported projects and meet with government counterparts, but above all, to see for myself what rural transformation has meant to rural people and to hear about their experiences from their own lips.

These have been without a doubt among the most rewarding parts of my tenure at IFAD. But these missions would not have been possible without the participation and hard work of numerous IFAD staff, both in Rome and in the field. I would like to acknowledge them here, because this book is informed by what I have learned and what I have seen in the countries where IFAD is investing in rural people.

For their direct support in the production of this volume I would like to acknowledge the following IFAD staff members: Henock Kifle, Bruce Murphy, Karen Zagor, Hazel Bedford, and Birgit Plockinger, as well as consultants Mark Foss and Adam Vincent.

1.

Dignity for all

In the beginning, Jane Njaguara – a farmer in Kenya – had a single goat. By the time I met her, she had poultry, cows, and a thriving milling business. Not only could she send her children to school, she was also employing others in the community. In other words, to echo the theme of this book, Jane had fetched her bucket of water.

Undoubtedly, many factors contributed to Jane's achievements, including her membership of a dairy group supported by an IFAD-supported project. But a development project can only provide opportunity; it is only a drop in the bucket. I suspect the reason for Jane's success had as much to do with an inner drive to provide a better life for her family.

In my career as both a scientist and an administrator, I have learned to track success through objective indicators. But I have also found that to understand results we must go beyond what can be measured in a test tube or plotted on a spreadsheet. In the end, development is about what really matters to people. It's about empowering them to take greater control of their lives, against all the odds that may be stacked against them.

Sometimes a project's success can be measured against tangible factors. For me, however, the most important outcomes are often intangible, such as the pride of a mother who can send her children to school well-fed and well-nourished, perhaps for the first time. When I am privileged to witness such a moment in people's lives I know that real change is possible.

On paper, the 2030 Agenda for Sustainable Development is a blueprint for ending hunger and undernutrition, as well as tackling poverty, inequality, and the impact of climate change (UN General Assembly, 2015b). There are 17 Sustainable Development Goals (SDGs), and 169 targets, indicators, and means of implementation. The Agenda also commits signatories to a 'robust, voluntary, effective, participatory, transparent and integrated follow-up and review framework' to ensure implementation over the next 15 years.

This level of rhetoric is necessary for such a sweeping and ambitious agreement. A detailed list of targets and indicators is also critical to keep us all on track and to help measure outcomes. Yet I do not want to lose sight of what's truly important about the SDGs.

Development is a measurable process aimed at delivering immeasurable goods – improvement in collective and individual well-being and a safer, fairer, and sustainable world. At its heart, then, the 2030 Agenda is about restoring and strengthening hope and dignity for people struggling to make better lives for themselves and their families.

Can such an ambitious agenda be achieved? My answer is: why not?

The international community achieved the first Millennium Development Goal (MDG) – to halve the poverty rate – five years ahead of schedule (UN, 2015). There are now more than 100 middle-income countries, as diverse as Brazil, Lesotho, and Vanuatu (World Bank n.d. a). Globally, 1.8 billion people are middle class, a number that could increase to 3.2 billion by 2020 and 4.9 billion by 2030 (Kharas, 2010). And in the last 15 years, the proportion of undernourished people in the developing world has fallen by almost half (FAO et al., 2015).

The 2030 Agenda and the SDGs reflect a growing consensus on development priorities, and signal the international community's desire to solve the world's problems. It is significant that this agenda was developed and agreed in a consultative process among the world's governments and ratified by world leaders. But the time has come to go beyond speeches and declarations, meetings and reports, and expression of commitments.

While we applaud the universal nature of the Agenda and the consultative process behind it, it is also important to recognize continuity with previous development efforts. We must be aware of the issues that have blocked their implementation so we can anticipate and, if possible, avoid similar problems. It is now more than ten years since the Paris Declaration on Aid Effectiveness called for greater country ownership, harmonization, and accountability. Much progress has been made towards these goals, even as the direction of official development assistance (ODA) has become more uncertain. The 2030 Agenda will require even more attention to harmonization, and in addition to being owned by countries, implementation will have to involve the very people we are trying to help. This is what people-centred development means.

At the same time, the growing role of private foundations, more public–private partnerships, South–South and triangular cooperation, and the potential to leverage billions of dollars in remittances for development, are all changing the way we think about development. Everywhere there is an intensifying focus on demonstrating impact and results, and showing value for money in development spending.

Far more than the MDGs, the 2030 Agenda is an ambitious agenda: it aims to eradicate poverty and hunger, to leave no one behind, and to put all economies and societies on a sustainable path. It is also comprehensive, spanning social, environmental, and economic issues, as well as issues related to governance and means of implementation. Finally, it is an integrated agenda, with progress on any goal requiring concurrent and coherent action around others.

We know what to do. We know what works and what doesn't work. What we now need is sustained, evidence-based action. The 2030 Agenda has raised the bar in terms of the ambitions of development; but the expectations have been raised as well. We will be held accountable for delivering tangible and verifiable results.

The importance of rural transformation

The 2030 Agenda is achievable if we recognize the multi-faceted and interconnected nature of the challenges.

Our world is full of paradoxes, some of them grotesque. Amid rising affluence in our world, there is also growing inequality. In 2015, some 836 million people still lived in poverty (UN, 2015), and 795 million people remained chronically undernourished (FAO et al., 2015). While these hundreds of millions go to bed hungry each night, a third of all food is lost or wasted (FAO, 2011a). The three-quarters of the world's poor who live in rural areas are responsible for up to 80 per cent of the food produced in sub-Saharan Africa and parts of Asia (IFAD, 2016c), yet many must buy food for their own table (Christiaensen and Demery, 2007).

It is a terrible irony that so many who produce food for others must buy it for themselves. But more than that, it is a travesty because smallholders are penalized at both ends. Lack of access to markets, poor infrastructure, and other causes often prevent smallholder farmers from benefiting from higher food prices.

At the same time, they must pay these high prices to feed their own families.

Against this backdrop, we must confront the question of how humanity will feed and sustain itself in the future. The world is becoming increasingly urban, yet cities are still fed by people working the land in rural areas. The health of urban dwellers depends on the quality of the water that flows into cities from rural areas. And without strong rural economies that offer decent jobs and dignified living conditions, the exodus to cities will continue unabated, creating social, economic, and environmental instability.

Given the lack of resources and access to markets faced by many rural people – especially women, who make up nearly half of the developing world's farmers – there is little incentive to improve yields and productivity. If farming is perceived as a back-breaking and unrewarding activity, it is hardly surprising that young people leave rural areas in search of opportunity, swelling already overcrowded cities. Who will feed the more than 9 billion people expected to inhabit our planet by 2050 (UN DESA, 2015).

Rural areas are changing, as higher returns from agriculture attract more investment and create new opportunities. More than incremental change, however, rural areas need transformation. In an ideal world, higher demand for food and higher prices would translate into greater income and prosperity for the people who work the world's 500 million small farms (IFAD, 2013g). It is not enough for investment to flow into local areas. Laws and regulations must be in place to safeguard smallholders' access to land and the rights of local people. Only in this way can we move towards true transformation.

Viewed in a single column, the 17 SDGs appear almost manageable – a kind of global 'to-do' list that we must simply work through, one item at a time. Reality, of course, is much messier. Cross-cutting issues weave below the surface of the SDGs, and we ignore them at our peril. We must make progress on all the SDGs at once, recognizing how our efforts in one area can support work in another.

I am heartened, for example, that SDG 1 aims to 'end poverty in all its forms everywhere' and SDG 2 to 'end hunger, achieve food security and improved nutrition and promote sustainable agriculture' (UN General Assembly, 2015b: 14). These goals, so critical to the lives of poor rural people, are at the 'top' of our collective to-do list. Yet I also know these goals are tied to a range of complex issues – from the inequalities faced by women to the causes of migration, or the impact of climate change.

While there is no single path to achieving the 2030 Agenda, I argue in this book that rural lives and rural development matter to the Agenda in a particular way. Any journey towards the SDGs must connect the smallholder farms in the countryside with the urban areas that rely on them for their survival and prosperity. Achieving such a universal agenda depends, paradoxically, on the individual journeys of millions of people out of hunger and poverty – each with a unique bucket of water to be filled.

Dramatic change is possible. Too many of the world's rural areas remain destitute, but over the years, in places as far-flung as Bangladesh and Burkina Faso, I have seen how rural transformation can change lives and communities. And this process must start with *small* farms.

The small family farm has been the main model of agriculture for thousands of years. In future, its role will only grow in importance. Therefore, we cannot leave the fate of smallholders to chance: they must be integrated coherently into development dialogue and planning.

When three-quarters of the world's poorest and hungriest people live in rural areas, they require a universal agenda to make these areas a priority. Simply put, recognizing the special needs of smallholders will go a long way towards rebalancing inequalities between rural and urban areas, and achieving all the SDGs.

There is also a practical reason to support small farms. In most of the developing world, the terrain and the socio-political structure are simply not conducive to larger farms. Developing the potential of smaller farms, then, is good economics because farming production systems have few economies of scale. In fact, small farms are often more productive, per hectare, than large farms when agro-ecological conditions and access to technology are comparable (Lerman and Sutton, 2006).

In China, 200 million small farms cultivate only 10 per cent of the world's agricultural land, yet they are responsible for 20 per cent of total production (HLPE, 2013). Over 10 million of Vietnam's rice farms are on fewer than 2 hectares of land (Thapa, 2009). These small-scale farmers are contributing to the success of one of the largest rice exporting countries.

Successful small farms lead to more vibrant rural economies. The impact on the local economy of more productive and remunerative small farms is to spur higher demand for locally produced goods and services. And this in turn spurs the growth of non-farm employment in services, agro-processing, and small-scale manufacturing. The net result is a dynamic flow of economic benefits between rural and urban areas so that nations have balanced and sustained growth. These are all keys to rural transformation.

Unlocking the potential

Transformation is not a new idea. More than 40 years ago, the 1974 World Food Conference recognized that food security and famine were the result of structural problems relating to poverty rather than failures in food production. The conference, which gave birth to IFAD, produced the far-reaching Universal Declaration on the

Eradication of Hunger and Malnutrition. It stated that 'to remove the obstacles to food production and to provide proper incentives to agricultural producers' would require 'effective measures of socio-economic transformation', including policy reform, 'the reorganization of rural structures', 'the encouragement of producer and consumer co-operatives', and 'the mobilization of the full potential of human resources, both male and female', in order to achieve 'integrated rural development and the involvement of small farmers, fishermen and landless workers' (World Food Conference General Assembly, 1974).

Four decades later, we need to take a fresh look at our expectations for transformation. As the cliché suggests, it is better to teach people to fish than to give them fish to eat. But a truly transformative agenda would set the bar much higher, addressing the whole context in which people fish, how they fish, and what they fish for. It helps them fish today in a way that ensures there will be fish to be caught tomorrow and years into the future.

At IFAD, we build the capacity of farmer groups and organizations because, when smallholders join together, they have greater purchasing power, greater bargaining power in the marketplace, and greater power to influence policies that affect their lives. But we also know that local people are a fountain of knowledge. They know the times of flooding, the areas most affected by water scarcity, and the crops and livestock that respond best during droughts. They may lack formal education, but their experience of their context far surpasses that of the development workers who parachute into a village for a few weeks or months. Local people know what they need in order to prosper.

It may not be enough to upgrade value chains through agricultural research and extension services. Smallholders also need access to finance to adopt new technologies or diversify their production and crop systems.

The development community increasingly realizes that smallholders are agents of change. Now the leaders and decision-makers of developing countries must get the message. Rural transformation requires governments to be responsible, transparent, and reliable. They must invest in their resources and their people more strategically. Ultimately, development starts at home.

In my own continent of Africa, only around 6 per cent of cultivated land is irrigated, compared with 38 per cent in Asia (FAO, 2005). And on average, sub-Saharan Africa applies only 18 kilograms of fertilizer per hectare of cultivated land compared to more than 149 kilograms in South Asia (World Bank, n.d. a).

Africa needs to scale up productivity, not necessarily by exploiting and expanding agricultural land, but by improving the productivity of existing land. Its leaders must invest more of their countries' own resources in agricultural research and development. They must reform their institutions to improve both the adoption and impact of agricultural innovation systems. And they must support the marriage of traditional technology with this culture of innovation.

As a Nigerian by birth, I grieve for the untapped potential of Africa. More than that, it symbolizes the mismanagement and corruption that has kept so many millions mired in hunger and poverty. Corruption is not by any means limited to Africa, but the scale of illicit outflows from the continent – some US$75 bn a year – is nothing short of scandalous (Kar and Spanjers, 2015). This money should be spent building roads, installing electrical lines, and educating and feeding people. Instead, the misappropriation of funds only feeds cynicism and despair.

At a time of global fiscal austerity, the use of foreign aid dollars attracts much scrutiny, and even criticism. Yet perhaps there is less attention to the fact that ODA accounts for less than US$132 bn of developing country budgets annually across the entire world (OECD, 2016). Cumulative domestic resources, on the other hand, are estimated at US$7 tn annually (World Bank, 2013). How well are these resources being managed? What is their impact on development objectives? A universal agenda also implies the need to take a holistic view on the resource side as well. And the agenda has to be universally owned; ODA may be inadequate to achieve the SDGs, but ODA is not the whole story.

Developing countries need responsible governments accountable to their people and not to their own pockets. They need visionary leaders committed to the rule of law and the rooting out of corruption and fiscal mismanagement. They need people empowered to make lasting, transformative changes in their lives and communities.

Poverty is not just a problem for individuals; it is a problem for societies. And since it is systemic, it requires systematic solutions. Hunger and poverty don't just happen; they are created – by inequality, lack of opportunity, neglect, and discrimination. This is why the 2030 Agenda rightly calls for an integrated approach to poverty, hunger, and food insecurity; one that addresses issues of rights, equality, inclusion, and good governance, alongside an economic and an environmental agenda.

Inequality is unsustainable for the human race; it produces hunger, poverty, and conflict. It defies the fundamental right to human dignity that people across the world find in work and well-being. It also hinders development, and insofar as it contributes to the continuation of unsustainable ways of living, it ultimately leads to the exhaustion of productive resources upon which human life depend.

A world in which unsustainable modes of food production and consumption have left hundreds of millions undernourished and poor and have done nothing to mitigate risks from unchecked climate change is not the future we want.

Yet we must be realistic. The future we want isn't free, and it isn't enough just to want it. It will have to be paid for – with greater investment in sustainable agriculture and rural development to ensure adequate, safe, and nutritious food for all, and by tearing down the barriers that prevent poor people from accessing food, inputs, finance, and myriad other essentials. It will cost us not just money, but time – and a higher level of care and attention. The cost of inaction, however, is higher still.

By working together, and committing to meet the 2030 Agenda, I believe we can not only ensure sustainable food and nutrition security, but also create a world where crisis is averted. I explore these ideas in more detail in the chapters that follow.

2.

Sowing conflict or growing peace?

Sustainable Development Goal (SDG) 16 deals with peace, justice, and inclusive institutions. Peace, stability, and the rule of law are important to establish the 'enabling environment' for successful inclusive development. But development also contributes to enhancing peace and security. About 40 per cent of IFAD's portfolio is in fragile states or situations (IFAD, Programme Management Department, 2013). We cannot wait for peace: we have to build peace through development.

I know first-hand the devastating consequences of fragility and conflict. As a young man, I was just about to begin my university studies when the Biafran War broke out. My family life and our community were swept up in the crisis and, as a result, my education had to be delayed by three years. But I finally entered a university campus the year my high school classmates were graduating from the University of Ibadan.

I was one of the lucky ones. After another three years, I had earned a second-class upper, the best in my department that year. It earned me a Ford Foundation scholarship to pursue graduate studies in entomology at Kansas State University in the City of Manhattan, Kansas, USA, where I found myself on a cold January day in 1972.

Having survived conflict, I am keenly aware of what it can do and how it devastates and destroys lives and nations. Conflicts sometimes seem to strike with the suddenness of earthquakes or typhoons. The difference is that they are human creations. That fact makes them both a terrible, tragic waste and something that we can – and must – do something about.

Not a day goes by that conflict does not rage in some part of the world. When people can't afford to eat because they can't make a decent living, they become desperate.

Over the past few years, rising food prices have sparked food riots in many countries and fuelled political instability. Given such events, it is hard to see how we can have any kind of security without food security first of all.

Equally, not a day goes by that some person, some family, or some community does not take a step towards filling their bucket of water – towards a better, more secure future, one free from conflict, hunger, and poverty. Today we are witnessing the greatest mass movement of people ever. Globally, in 2015, 247 million migrants had left their homes for another country (World Bank, Migration and Remittances Team, Development Prospects Group, 2015). And the numbers are rising. In the Mediterranean alone, more than 76,000 migrants and refugees made their way to Europe in the first six weeks of 2016 – nearly 10 times more than the previous year over the same period (IOM, 2016).

What causes people to migrate? Conflict, certainly, but hunger, poverty, inequality, poor governance, persistent indignity, and lack of opportunity are also some of the drivers. Whether they are escaping a natural disaster or a crisis brought on by human action, the desperation of migrants is all too real. So real they can put aside the immense risk, convinced they will be the ones to succeed.

In recent years, forced displacement has become a global problem of unprecedented scale. In 2015, the number of people displaced by conflict and persecution surpassed 65 million, an all-time high (Edwards, 2016). Much of this movement is concentrated in the Near East and North Africa region, where conflict and violence affect Iraq, Syria, Yemen, and neighbouring countries – a region with a total population of concern of some 22 million people.

Many of these displaced people originate in rural areas, which leads to a collapse of food production. Further, rather than landing in formal camps, most displaced people end up staying in host communities, most often in rural areas. This can add pressure on natural resources, food security, and agricultural systems in host communities. In both instances, forced displacement has a strong rural dimension. In the short term, people in crisis need relief and emergency services; in the long term, communities and countries in crisis need development strategies that solve underlying problems.

There is a sometimes little appreciated connection between rural and urban issues. For example, the social upheaval in Tunisia had its roots deep in rural areas, in reaction to the inequalities between the coastal areas and the relatively marginalized interior. The establishment of a democratic climate in the country has led to demands for employment and infrastructure to meet basic needs within Tunisia's poorest regions.

IFAD deployed more resources to cover the unmet needs of rural people living in priority areas with a high incidence of poverty. One project approved in 2014, for example, aims to improve production conditions for sheep and goats, as well as encourage small livestock breeders and smallholder farmers to develop markets for camel milk. The project also supports small income-generating projects and microenterprises developed by young people and women (IFAD Operations, n.d. a).

Climate change

Climate change is another driver of migration, hunger, and instability. Imagine farmers whose yields are steadily dropping due to severely degraded soil or drought, or perhaps a month's worth of rain falls in a single day, drowning out hopes for a good harvest. In the face of inconsistent and extreme weather that makes it difficult to earn a living, who can blame farmers for migrating to the city or to another country that seems better off?

Long before the current crisis in Syria, researchers linked violent uprisings in the country during 2011 to the drought (Kelley et al., 2015). In fact, a three-year drought preceded the 'Arab awakening' of 2011, pushing wheat and bread prices in the region ever higher. In Syria, the period was marked by the migration of farmers to the cities.

Research has also shown a strong correlation between changes in global climate and civil conflict in sub-Saharan Africa (Burke, 2009). This certainly applies to Somalia, where livestock price shocks related to drought fuel conflicts by reducing the opportunity costs of fighting. Endemic poverty and lack of public safety nets, credit, and insurance make it difficult for people to cope when crisis strikes. Preliminary studies also indicate that helping people diversify their income and adapt to climate change and drought can strengthen their resilience to the effects of conflict and – significantly – also help prevent conflict.

In November 2015, in a report called *Shock Waves: Managing the Impacts of Climate Change on Poverty*, the World Bank warned that climate change may push more than 100 million people back into poverty over the next 15 years (Hallegate, 2015). It also identified sub-Saharan African and South Asia – the poorest regions of the world – as the hardest hit. In response, it called for both mitigation and adaptation efforts to protect the poor.

Targeted action, such as early warning systems, flood protection, and heat-resistant crops, can help poor rural people build resilience to climate shocks. Without such coping mechanisms, smallholders may leave their villages, migrating to urban areas or even to other countries in the hope of building a better future elsewhere.

The people focus: understanding context

Success in rural development requires the combination of creativity with long-term commitment, especially in areas plagued by some form of conflict. The nature of conflict is not always full-blown or even visible to the naked eye. It can exist at various degrees and intensities, and its negative effects can be persistent and stubborn.

One of IFAD's most encouraging successes in a conflict-laden community was the Northern Areas Development Project (NADP) in Pakistan, which started in 1998. The project brought new roads, clean water, new crops and livestock, and literacy to an area previously unreached by development efforts. In addition, 140 women's organizations were formed and women began starting small businesses.

But it was not easy. At first, people offered strong resistance, even violent resistance, to the project. Some aspects – such as microfinance – were viewed as a threat to the community's traditions and religion.

There were also issues of conflict that extended beyond the community. According to Imam Maulana Muzzamil Shah, 'Before, people from this area would go and train in different areas of Pakistan in the name of waging jihad to protect Islam. After the project, a change came on the people, and they stopped going. Now nobody goes' (Nwanze, 2012a: 6).

It was a long process for the project to be accepted. Once people realized the project was not there to attack Islam, development was embraced and extremism was rejected. Time and again, IFAD's experience has shown that sensitivity to context and engagement and dialogue with local people and their organizations are critical to success.

If we create programmes that help people overcome the barriers to their own development, we reduce the appeal of violent and destructive responses to conditions that are, admittedly, intolerable. In so doing, we give them a way to fight poverty and hunger instead of each other.

In the state of Jharkland in India, many villages can only be reached on foot. Basic services and infrastructure are almost non-existent. Rural people have often been exploited by extremist groups and by moneylenders. Financed by IFAD and implemented by the Jharkhand Tribal Development Society and non-governmental partners, a project targeted 74,000 tribal households scattered through 180 villages in four districts (Chhattisgarh Tribal Development Programme, n.d.). Taking an integrated natural resource management approach, it dug ponds and wells, levelled fields, helped many families cultivate paddies, and encouraged them to add a second crop to generate income.

The project has been fully owned by the people themselves. Community discussion on agricultural and other local issues has increased in the Gram Sabha, the traditional forum of community self-government. Moreover, through creating self-help groups and building community awareness, the project has empowered women. Significantly, there have not been further disturbances in the programme areas since the project started work.

Staying the course

People tend to assume that when conflict breaks out, development ends. But even in countries like Syria and Yemen, poor rural people are trying to get on with their daily lives. As long as the rain falls and the sun shines, farmers will try to farm. When the conflict ends, a nation will rebuild more quickly if its agricultural system is more or less intact.

In an IFAD-supported project in Yemen, around 5,000 women and men took part in community-led advisory services (IFAD, Near East, North Africa and Europe Division, Programme Management Department, 2013). These introduced new crop varieties and drip irrigation in one of the country's poorest and most insecure governorates. Women invested their own money in a domestic water scheme, which reduces time spent collecting water by up to 300 hours a year. Participants reported a significant reduction in violent conflict in project areas, while evaluations have found considerable improvement in household food security and reduced rates of child malnutrition.

Despite the conflict in Syria, IFAD successfully completed four projects in recent years, improving livestock management and ensuring poor rural women and men had access to microfinance. The creation of revolving funds known as *sanadiq*, or 'savings boxes', gave entrepreneurs much easier access to microloans. By 2014, the projects had reached more than 24,000 beneficiaries, including 10,500 rural women, with a loan repayment rate of 100 per cent. Two years later, despite the country's turmoil, much of the nearly 130 *sanadiq* network was still operational, and small farmers and their families were still benefiting.

In some countries, the deep-rooted nature of the conflict requires greater patience, determination, and commitment to achieve results. For any number of reasons, change may be slow to take hold. Momentum gained during periods of stability may be undercut by renewed tension or violence. By continuing activities in the face of insecurity, IFAD can help communities maintain normality.

In Burundi, for example, IFAD remained active throughout the civil war that ravaged the country between 1993 and 2006. After the armed conflict ended, we were the first development partner to move into the areas that had been hardest hit. We provided support to reconstruct rural infrastructure and the damaged agricultural sector, while also helping to build stronger communities and lay the foundations for a more cohesive, democratic society.

Four IFAD-supported projects focused on rebuilding rural livelihoods across the country, but the Transitional Programme of Post-Conflict Reconstruction (TPPCR), first launched in March 2006, took on the task of peacebuilding more broadly. TPPCR undertook community development, legal issues, HIV/AIDS awareness, support to food production, animal solidarity chains, rural infrastructure development, and literacy activities. The approach helped build lasting democratic institutions by addressing health and education issues. In so doing, it struck at the roots of civil conflict: poverty, lack of opportunity, lack of education, lack of a future. If left untreated, these problems can lead to desperation.

By 2012, project activities were enabling people not only to rebuild their lives, but also to prosper. The introduction of the system of rice intensification (SRI) allowed farmers to more than double their rice yields per hectare. Lives and communities had a future again. Nicaise Arakaza, a young man from Burambi, put it this way, 'In the past it was all about vengeance ... The programme helped us to learn good governance. It taught us the codes of law. Now we know how to resolve conflicts.

You can explain your problem and find a peaceful resolution' (Nwanze, 2012a).

IFAD is not only raising community awareness about legal processes in Burundi, but also promoting gender equality by helping women pursue justice through the courts. As is often the case, education plays a vital role. Literacy classes are enabling women to read legal documents before signing them, particularly those relating to ownership of land, and ensure that their rights are respected.

Since those optimistic days following the conflict, Burundi has descended into more uncertainty. By the spring of 2016, more than 260,000 people had crossed into neighbouring countries seeking refuge from the political unrest (USAID, 2016). At its heart, it is the desperate need for land that is fuelling conflict in the country, and IFAD believes that greater investment in agriculture can help nurture peace.

In 2016, we approved a flexible programming strategy for the country, one that we can adapt based on the political situation (IFAD Operations, n.d. c). For us, the most important thing is to maintain a presence there. Even in difficult situations, it is important to find solutions to maintain infrastructure and activities initiated by the local population with project support. This kind of support promotes sustainability and helps prepare for the post-conflict phase.

Many fragile countries or areas have experienced cycles of development and conflict, in which schools and clinics that take months or years to build are burnt or destroyed in a few hours. Development partners flee; they return after the flames of conflict have died down, sometimes years later, but too often the cycle begins again. In many cases IFAD has stayed behind, continuing its projects whenever possible, because we know that conflict often grows out of long-term problems and demands long-term solutions.

Some of the populations that participate in IFAD-supported programmes are among the poorest people on earth. It is not surprising that agricultural development is the most powerful engine of poverty reduction in developing countries. Indeed, gross domestic product (GDP) growth generated by agriculture is at least four times as effective in reducing poverty as growth in other sectors.

But reducing poverty must be about more than adding to GDP. To transform communities, rural development must address a range of social dimensions, and even the environmental context with which rural people must contend. We often talk of creating a climate for investment; we should also try to create a climate of peace.

It is a mistake to assume that development activities will necessarily lead to peace. There are even cases in which interventions can provoke tension and conflict within communities or households. In some countries, for example, studies have shown that when a crop produced for household consumption becomes marketable, men take control over its production and reap the profits.

The key lesson from all of this: no one country is the same as another – and no country stays the same very long. The ground is constantly shifting beneath our feet. Development practitioners must be nimble, ready to shift focus depending on people's needs. Further, they must remember the impact of conflict will be hardest on vulnerable groups, including women. Unless we become aware of gender relations, initiatives could disproportionately benefit men.

Programme design requires careful targeting and a clear appreciation of the risks of trying to grow peace and development in unpromising soil. Of course, there are places where security is so fragile that undertaking development activities would be foolhardy and even irresponsible.

The same conditions that provide fertile ground for unrest and conflict also create an urgent moral imperative for development: gross injustice; severe disparities in opportunity; lack of infrastructure and the tools to make life better; poor governance and corruption; intense competition for resources; greed; and lack of access to education or credit. Remove the obstacles and provide the tools, and people will begin to build a better world around themselves.

Extreme weather conditions, severe drought and crop failure, massive internal migration and forced displacement, civil unrest, and political destabilization are all connected, and all impinge on agriculture and rural development. But as the examples show, the contrary is also true. Sustainable rural development can ensure food security, help farmers adapt to climate change, and build stable communities.

Both conflict and development are driven by a profound dissatisfaction with the way things are. One is a destructive response, while the other is positive and constructive. Crucially, both can happen in one and the same place. Resolving issues can be a way for a nation to avoid conflict or to heal from it more quickly.

Waiting for peace to take root before we begin to nurture development is a luxury we cannot afford. If we want to help rural women and men raise themselves out of poverty and food insecurity, we have to go to where they are. They may be in least developed countries, fragile states, or pockets of intractable poverty in middle-income countries. Poverty finds the vulnerable wherever they are, and so must we.

Experience has shown that by forging partnerships with rural people and letting them take charge of their own futures, change is rooted more firmly in the community. A transformation occurs. The process begins by listening to rural people, working with them, and building their organizations.

There are both practical and moral arguments for community-led, people-centred development. Interventions driven by external actors may fail for any number of reasons. They may be inappropriate to the context, for example. The very fact that they are imposed from outside can also be enough to invalidate them. Inclusiveness is not simply a question of respect and dignity – it also makes sense, and will lead to better results.

No one should go to sleep hungry. No one should see a child's potential wither under malnutrition, illiteracy, and hopelessness. No woman should be denied access to resources just because she is not a man. No one should be denied a voice simply because it suits someone else to keep them silent.

Our goal must be to promote hope instead of hate – to see communities brought together to overcome adversity, not split apart by it. When we approach rural communities, we must look not only at what they are, but what they could be – and what they want to be.

3.

Farming as a business

When I insisted for many years that small-scale farms were as much businesses as large-scale operations, my views were considered at best romantic and at worst foolish. Never mind that 500 million smallholder farms around the world provide livelihoods for more than 2 billion people and produce about 80 per cent of the food in Asia and sub-Saharan Africa. Few senior business or government leaders seriously believed that farmers working small plots of land could be considered part of the 'business community'.

Today, the concept of smallholder farms as a business has become commonplace – and not a moment too soon. I was surprised and delighted at a recent conference on Africa where smallholder farmers were described as the largest private sector group in African agriculture. By 2050, according to projections, well over 9 billion people will be living on our planet. Our finite resources are already under pressure from climate change, urbanization – and a rapidly growing population. How will we cope with all these new mouths to feed?

The sheer scope of the challenge would seem to demand grand solutions. Perhaps the world requires larger and more heavily mechanized farms that can generate the much-needed food. The efficiency of modern tractors working large-scale farms may strike many as the obvious answer.

Yet this is not the case. In Brazil, for example, small farmers using mixed cropping on 8-hectare plots generate one job, while large-scale mechanized monocultures take 67 hectares to create one job. In other words, small farms are eight times more effective at job creation (FAO, 2012b). Supporting smallholder agriculture, then, is not a romantic notion of doing good for the poor. It makes good business sense.

Indeed, there is no reason why small- and medium-sized farms cannot contribute to a stable food supply in the developed and developing world alike. The agri-food sector already represents US$5 tn (Goedde et al., 2015). Smallholder farmers thus have a huge opportunity to increase their business, escape poverty, and achieve food security.

I would go still further, arguing that smallholders are the key to global food security. Turning smallholder farmers into profitable rural businesses that generate surpluses is not only the best way to achieve global food security; it also offers a path out of poverty and hunger. Frankly, the only reason why small farms cannot play a critical role in feeding the world is our own failure to help them do it.

Too often the people who grow the food go hungry themselves. Their inability to feed themselves is not a reflection on their capacities to farm the land or operate a business. Rather, it speaks to the lack of opportunities and resources that leave them few options to improve their lives. If we don't work harder to help rural people live better lives, we will all suffer.

We need our rural areas today. In future, we will need them even more – to grow more food and to maintain our ecosystems that help provide clean air and water. By making it possible for smallholders to invest in their businesses, we can improve income, food security, and nutrition.

More than that, we can transform rural areas into spaces where people can earn dignified and decent livings. Given the symbiotic relationship between rural and urban areas, an investment in the prosperity of smallholders will have a multiplying effect – ensuring the flow of food and services into towns and cities, while helping ensure that urbanization is also sustainable.

The idea that large-scale, input-intensive agriculture is the answer to future food needs may still have its adherents. But this approach is increasingly understood to be problematic. It is highly significant that the Sustainable Development Goals include a dedicated target on smallholder agriculture. Specifically, Target 2.3 calls for the world to 'double the agricultural productivity and incomes of small-scale food producers, in particular women, indigenous peoples, family farmers, pastoralists and fishers, including through secure and equal access to land, other productive resources and inputs, knowledge, financial services, markets and opportunities for value addition and non-farm employment' (UN General Assembly, 2015b). Reaching the target through scaled-up and appropriate investment is the next urgent step.

The needs of smallholder farmers in developing countries are not so very different from those of large farmers in developed countries. They require access to inputs and financial services, paved roads to get their goods to market, and processing and storage for what they don't sell immediately after harvest.

But they also need what much of the developed world takes for granted: clean water; reliable electricity; an internet connection that can provide information and generate knowledge; secure access to their land; access to credit and other resources; safety nets to mitigate risk; and an overall enabling policy environment.

Too often they don't have these things. Consequently, smallholders are unable to exploit their full potential. They cannot be productive.

Let me unpack some of these issues, starting with land tenure.

Land tenure

Land is fundamental to the lives of poor rural people as a source of food, shelter, income, and social identity. Whether farmers own their land affects what crops they choose to grow and whether they grow them for subsistence or commercial purposes. It also influences the extent to which farmers are prepared to invest – financially and emotionally – in the long-term well-being of their land, or adopt new technologies and innovations. As an added benefit, tenure security also allows people to diversify their livelihoods by using their land as collateral, renting it out, or selling it.

Yet, in rural communities, the poorest people often have weak or unprotected tenure rights. Women can be particularly vulnerable. If they obtain land through kinship relationships with men or marriage, they may lose land rights if those family or legal ties are severed.

Paradoxically, development projects can make the problem worse. A project that introduces irrigation into rain-fed farmland, for example, can quickly change the economic and social dynamics of a community. Land farmed by smallholders once considered undesirable can suddenly attract the interest of more powerful settlers.

In recent years, public and private corporations have been investing in millions of hectares of land in Africa, Asia, and Latin America to produce food or biofuels. This land offers developing countries an opportunity to attract foreign and domestic investment that raises agricultural productivity, but it also brings a potential threat to the land rights of small-scale producers and indigenous communities.

IFAD supports investment by smallholder farmers, pastoralists, and indigenous peoples in their own production systems. It works with partners to identify alternative business models that can strengthen land and natural resource rights and boost agricultural development. These alternative ways of structuring agricultural investments include different types of contract farming schemes, joint ventures, management contracts, and new supply chain relationships.

In Burkina Faso and Mali, for example, smallholder farmers have partnered with Mali Biocarburant SA (MBSA) in a combination of a joint venture and contract farming (IFAD, n.d b). The company produces non-polluting biodiesel from jatropha, a crop grown for energy rather than food. Farmers plant and harvest jatropha and their cooperatives sell the jatropha nuts to MBSA, which extracts the oil. This biofuel model integrates jatropha production into the smallholder farming system without creating a conflict between food and fuel production because jatropha is either intercropped with food crops or grown on unproductive land.

Overall, MBSA works with more than 10,000 smallholder farmers in three regions in Mali and two regions in Burkina Faso. The farmers take an active role in the company, participating in price agreements and decision-making processes, and benefiting from increased sales of jatropha nuts. As shareholders, they also benefit from increased value of shares and dividends. Furthermore, land rights have been maintained, yields of food crops planted alongside jatropha have improved, and incomes are diversified – which provides a safety net should other crops fail.

These efforts to promote land tenure security – for both women and men – are an important step on the road to reducing rural poverty. Secure access to land means that people in rural areas are less vulnerable to hunger and poverty. Even when land is classified as communal, under-utilized or marginal, it may provide a vital base for the livelihoods of poor people who use it for crop farming, herding, or collecting fuelwood or medicines. In other words, access to land can set in motion opportunities for smallholder farmers to develop businesses. In Chapter 7, I reflect on the role of national governments in creating land use policies that protect smallholders.

Inputs

What good is land without the right external inputs – such as seeds, fertilizers, pesticides, and water – to make it productive?

In many cases, poor farmers face enormous difficulties accessing improved seeds. When they do, their yields are frequently below potential. In sub-Saharan Africa, to take an extreme example, the gap between potential and actual yields of maize is as much as 200 per cent (Koo, 2013). Much needs to be done to improve farmers' access to improved seed of all sorts, and to help them realize their full productive potential.

Similarly, farmers in sub-Saharan Africa use less than 18 kilograms of fertilizer per hectare compared with about 88 kilograms in the Middle East and North Africa, and 246 kilograms in East Asia and the Pacific (World Bank, n.d. a). Small increases in organic or inorganic fertilizer in the region could produce dramatic improvements in yields.

In all regions of the developing world, farmers need to make more efficient use of resources, especially water. Only about 6 per cent of total cultivated land in Africa is irrigated, compared with 37 per cent in Asia (IFAD, 2014). Estimates suggest that irrigation alone could increase output by up to 50 per cent in Africa (You et al., 2011).

Each region has its particular challenges, but sustainable agricultural intensification holds out the promise of using resources – especially water – more efficiently. Over the past few decades, farmers have taken up a growing number of intensification practices, some building on traditional techniques. Emerging practices use external inputs more selectively, striving to maximize synergies within the farm cycle while adapting to climate change. They typically aim to improve soil fertility, structure and water-retaining capacity, utilizing a combination of organic, biological, and mineral resources, and using water more sparingly and efficiently.

Given the right market conditions, sustainable agricultural intensification can enhance the productivity of smallholders, enabling them to make the most effective use of local resources, and helping to build resilience to climate stress and deliver environmental services, including some linked to climate change mitigation.

Storage

And there are post-production challenges as well. What good are greater yields when farmers have no place to store the surplus harvest securely?

In sub-Saharan Africa, between 20 to 40 per cent of crops are lost because of deterioration post harvest (Kaminski and Christiaensen, 2014). These losses are scandalous, particularly on a continent where millions go hungry (FAO, IFAD, and WFP, 2015). But post-harvest losses occur across the developing world, and affect the motivation of farmers to enhance productivity. Smallholders want to grow more – to move beyond subsistence to surplus – but only if the ends justify the hard work.

In Timor-Leste, farmers like to say there are three seasons: wet, dry, and hungry. For three months of the year, households can go without staples such as rice or maize. In such an environment, IFAD imagined that smallholders would be eager to improve productivity through higher maize seeds. Yet the farmers were indifferent or sceptical. They were losing 30 per cent or more of their stored maize to rodents and weevils (IFAD, 2011b). Of what value was a surplus under these conditions?

IFAD teamed up with the Timor-Leste Ministry of Agriculture and Fisheries and the Australian Government to provide better storage, as well as better seeds. This partnership brought together an existing IFAD-financed project on storage technology with an existing Australian project for seed production and research (ibid.).

Working together, the partners aimed to increase food availability by as much as 70 per cent through a combination of better yields and lower post-harvest losses. The secure storage is an incentive for farmers to adopt high-yielding varieties, and should allow them to wait for the off-seasons to sell their surplus, when prices are higher.

In other cases, IFAD has helped farmers adopt best practices for post-harvest drying or cooling and storage. These include access to climate information services to manage drying and cooling processes more effectively, and improved storage methods, such as hermetically sealed bags and enough pallets to keep produce off the floor and well ventilated. Storage facilities must also be strong enough to withstand high winds and intense rain. These techniques may not win awards for innovation, but as I argue in Chapter 8, small ideas are sometimes more than enough to meet a pressing need.

Infrastructure

Having enhanced productivity and cut post-harvest losses, smallholder farmers would seem well on the way to selling their surplus. First, though, they have to reach the market. Too often, this proves to be an almost insurmountable task.

In sub-Saharan Africa, a third of farmers live more than five hours from a market town of 5,000 people (Livingston et al., 2011). Across the continent, badly maintained roads are the norm. This is no way to develop markets or to create the jobs and conditions that will transform rural communities. For many millions of farmers, the inaccessibility of markets is literally a roadblock to better food and nutrition security.

We must ensure sufficient investment in rural infrastructure with paved roads and adequate affordable transportation so that farmers can sell at a competitive price and still make a profit. Complementary strategies can also reduce the cost of shipping.

A good illustration of this is cassava, a crop that is made up of nearly 70 per cent water, making it easy to spoil, and bulky and expensive to transport. It is a staple food upon which hundreds of millions of Africans depend. And with good processing, cassava can be transformed into animal feed, flour, industrial starch, sorbitol and other products that increase potential markets, all while increasing shelf life and reducing transport costs.

Markets

Once they get their goods to market, will smallholders receive fair value for their labour? Knowledge is power. With better information and connections, smallholders can protect their interests more effectively.

Poor rural producers and their goods are connected to markets within larger agricultural value chains. Studies confirm that producers often earn significantly less than other actors in the chain. Coffee growers in Uganda, for example, were earning just 0.5 per cent of the retail price to consumers in London. For fresh vegetables grown in Africa for export to Europe, about 27 per cent of the final price went to the retailer, while producers earned just 12 per cent for *mangetout* peas grown in Zimbabwe and 14 per cent for vegetables grown in Kenya (IFAD, 2012a).

To successfully intervene in a value chain to the benefit of poor rural producers, it is important to understand and take account of the distribution of power and control among the various actors. This means recognizing how much influence producers can have over the quantity, quality, and prices within the chain. Different types of chain and different degrees of farmer organization provide different outcomes in terms of producer prices.

Intervening along the value chain often means enabling poor rural people to 'move up' the chain and capture margins previously caught by other players, including wholesalers, processors, and exporters. When the links between production, processing, marketing, and consumption are aligned for smallholders, wonderful things can happen.

In Egypt, before smallholders could move up the value chain, they had to transform a barren desert into land that could support market-oriented agriculture. The IFAD-supported West Noubaria Rural Development Project introduced a credit fund, systems for sewage and refuse disposal, and drip irrigation. It also trained the farmers in crop and livestock production and in sustainable water and land management techniques (IFAD Operations, n.d. f).

The project proved a boon – not just for existing farmers, but for youth who were struggling to make a living. Ahmad Abdelmunem Al-Far, for example, had a degree in agricultural engineering from Cairo University, but like many other Egyptian graduates, he was unable to find work in his profession after graduation. After years of unemployment, except for occasional work in a garage or as a waiter, he responded to an announcement offering farming opportunities to unemployed graduates.

Like other farmers, Ahmad received a plot of 2.1 hectares of newly reclaimed desert. He and his wife began cultivating fava beans, onions, green peppers, tomatoes, and potatoes. They bought cows for meat, cheese, butter, ghee, yogurt, and fresh milk. And they planted oranges, which have become a cash crop.

All told, some 36,000 participating farmers began supplying fresh oranges and authentic mozzarella cheese to the resorts of Egypt's Sharm-el-Sheikh. They exported sweet peppers and sun-dried tomatoes to Italy and the United States, peanuts to Germany and Switzerland, and raisins, artichokes, apricots, peaches, and potatoes to a variety of European countries.

Perhaps their most impressive contract is with Heinz, which agreed to buy more than 6,000 tons of tomatoes each year from 300 project farms. Heinz provides the farmers with seeds and guarantees to buy half their harvest at an agreed price. If the farmers cannot sell the remaining tomatoes in the domestic market, Heinz is committed to buying them, too.

There are many paths to prosperity through farming. For example, with consumers in developed countries increasingly concerned about the origins of their food, smallholders can seize emerging opportunities. With a little imagination, 'obscure' grains and cereals may be able to find new markets.

Teff, for example, has been grown in Ethiopia for thousands of years. It is a key ingredient in making *injera*, the traditional flatbread. This tiny grain is high in fibre, protein, and iron. Perhaps most critically, it is gluten-free, perfectly suited to meet growing demand for wheat-free products in western markets (IFADTV, 2016a).

Why couldn't teff follow the same path to global success as quinoa? Once considered a 'poor man's food' in Bolivia, quinoa – a member of the spinach family – has become chic in the western world as a health food. Its newfound popularity and its higher nutritional value add up to improved livelihoods, food security, and nutrition. This has been a boon to smallholder farmers who contend with a harsh climate and few livelihood options.

Ironically, many Bolivians are still conscious of the stigma associated with quinoa and prefer to eat imported grains. But this, too, is slowly changing. An IFAD-supported project is helping promote quinoa as an alternative to less nutritious imports (IFADTV, 2013). It specifically targets Bolivian farmers who don't produce enough quinoa to supply export markets, but who can supply local food stores, bakeries, and restaurants. As they learn more about the nutritional value of quinoa, these farmers are also eating more of it themselves.

Access to finance

Farmers may have opportunities to expand beyond subsistence-level agriculture, and the will to do so, but how can they get ahead without money for investment? To operate commercially, farmers need access to finance and credit. For too many, however, these essential services remain – figuratively and literally – out of reach.

Not only does lack of finance hurt smallholders, it also undermines attempts to lift rural areas out of poverty. Ultimately, it is the investments of millions of rural micro, small and medium enterprises (MSMEs) that will primarily drive the transformation we want to see in rural areas across the world. By using domestic and international public funds in innovative ways to leverage these investments, we can achieve a large-scale and lasting impact on poverty and hunger reduction. In the process, we can create a world where more families live in dignity and young people realize their aspirations for a better life in their own rural communities.

The mobilization of development finance – including financial inclusion for vulnerable smallholders – has been recognized as a critical factor in the achievement of the 2030 Agenda. Sustainable Development Goal (SDG) 8, related to inclusive and sustainable growth, includes a target on support to entrepreneurship and access to financial services by MSMEs, and another related to strengthening institutional capacity to foster financial inclusion. Financial inclusion also features in SDG 1 in relation to the eradication of poverty (Target 1.4) (UN General Assembly, 2015b).

This issue took centre stage at the Third International Conference on Financing for Development in Addis Ababa, Ethiopia, held in 2015. The conference outcome – the Addis Ababa Agenda for Action (AAAA) – recognized agriculture, food security and nutrition, and support to MSMEs as areas where increased financing and investment could yield cross-cutting benefits for sustainable development (UN General Assembly, 2015a). It also recognized IFAD's valuable experience in this area.

It is estimated that most of the 2.5 billion people in the world who lack access to formal finance reside in rural areas, where agriculture provides the majority of livelihoods (IFAD, 2015c). Even among smallholders, access to finance can vary significantly depending on location, gender, degree of commercial orientation of the farm, product specialization, and type of value chain in which a farm participates. While each farmer's situation is unique, many face several common constraints to accessing finance, including poverty, lack of collateral and credit history, lack of legal status, isolation from banks, and irregular cash flow.

Multilateral development banks, including IFAD, have rich experience in addressing these challenges. In recent years, this has revolved around building the capacity of rural financial institutions and helping them network with other key players. In Nigeria, for example, IFAD has worked with the government to develop local microfinance institutions and link them to formal financial institutions (IFAD Operations, n.d. d). At the same time, we have helped enhance the accessibility of financial services for poor rural people – notably women – to raise their productivity as farmers and MSME operators.

With its sister agencies in Rome – the Food and Agriculture Organization of the United Nations and the World Food Programme – IFAD has also teamed up with Her Majesty Queen Máxima of the Netherlands in her capacity as the UN Secretary-General's Special Advocate for Inclusive Finance for Development

(UNSGSA). Together, we are raising awareness of how access to financial services – such as bank accounts, short-term credit, small loans, savings, and insurance – can help improve the lives and livelihoods of smallholder farmers and the rural poor (IFAD Newsroom, 2013).

In addition, IFAD is a member of the Consultative Group to Assist the Poor (CGAP), a global partnership of some 40 leading organizations that seek to advance financial inclusion. IFAD's partnership with CGAP offers a number of important avenues for technical exchange and allows for more effective dissemination of knowledge and experience in rural finance. Membership in CGAP has also enabled IFAD to benefit from advisory services, including participation in technical review committees, joint publication of case studies in rural finance, Microfinance Donor Peer Reviews, and the 2009 SmartAid for Microfinance Index.

CGAP has worked hard to develop emerging digital technologies that can make financial services more accessible to smallholders (CGAP, n.d.). Through mobile money accounts, for example, smallholders can send and receive money and make payments with participating merchants. They can access a bank savings account through their mobile phones, pay loans, claim insurance payments, and receive remittances from abroad (IFAD, Policy and Technical Advisory Division, 2016a).

These services are blossoming all over the world. For example, in Africa, mobile phone networks are bypassing fixed-line phone networks, which have remained limited and therefore are inadequate to spur rural transformation. Smallholder farmers in Ghana selling rice to the Ghana Agricultural Development Company, for example, can now receive payment in their Tigo Cash mobile wallets (Babcock, 2015). Coffee and cotton farmers in Uganda and the United Republic of Tanzania can receive payments from intermediaries through a SmartMoney mobile money application (ibid.). And cashew farmers in Madagascar can be paid through Airtel mobile money accounts (Riquet, 2013).

In Zimbabwe, Econet offers a package consisting of credit for agricultural inputs, loan payment reminders, and tips on using inputs like fertilizer (Mattern and Tarazi, 2015). In Kenya, through the Vodaphone group, M-PESA has transformed business practices for pastoralists and livestock traders in rural areas, allowing them to make quick and easy payments to both individuals and businesses (Reinke and Sperandini, 2012). Meanwhile, Vodaphone in Turkey offers a virtual marketplace for subscribers, enabling farmers to advertise their products (GSMA Intelligence, 2015).

While such services can be safe, efficient, and convenient, the reach of these technologies is still relatively limited. Moreover, illiteracy, mistrust, lack of transparent fees, and other factors may hinder their uptake. New technologies, then, are not a panacea for smallholders. But they are a potent business tool to support their livelihoods and help them rise above poverty.

Risk management

Risk management is another part of building smallholder resilience, helping them to become viable businesses. When a family no longer fears it can feed itself, it can diversify its crops to sell to the market. When the interest rate on a loan is 20 per cent rather than 200 per cent, a farmer can invest in fertilizer or farm equipment. When a farmer has a secure contract with a credible buyer, she will take the time to improve the quality of her produce.

In partnership with the World Food Programme, IFAD supports risk management instruments in developing countries, notably through weather index-based insurance, an insurance product correlated to weather patterns for local crops. Taking the next step, IFAD began hosting the multi-donor Platform for Agricultural

Risk Management (PARM) to promote risk management capacity for the agriculture sector in developing countries (Platform for Agricultural Risk Management, n.d.). It offers a holistic perspective to risk assessment, capacity building, and product development.

Many developing countries are also creating social protection programmes to build safety nets. Social protection is not only intrinsically important; it can also facilitate investment among rural households. Moreover, it can cushion the impact of price spikes on consumers. It is a valid alternative to policies that, in order to protect them in the short term, hinder the transmission of price increases to producers. Conditional cash transfers, for instance, are widespread in Latin America; they typically target poor families and seek to combine short-term poverty alleviation or improved nutrition with the long-term objective of breaking the cycle of intergenerational poverty by making transfers conditional on school attendance or the immunization of children.

Other programmes are based on employment guarantee and public works schemes, such as India's National Rural Employment Guarantee Act and Ethiopia's Productive Safety Net Programme, both of which provide part-time employment to millions of poor rural people.

Strong organizations, strong partnerships

Once farmers have land, seeds, finance, technology, and safety nets, they need partnerships to create strength in numbers.

Belonging to a strong farmers' organization allows smallholder farmers to bulk produce, reduce costs through economies of scale, and, perhaps most importantly, to strengthen their bargaining power with intermediaries and powerful private-sector actors. Membership can also bring access to financial, processing, and business services, all of which are key to empowering farmers to deal with the private sector on a more level playing field.

In Egypt, the Agrofood Group collaborates with farmers' associations to provide smallholder family farmers with training and high quality seeds so they can meet strict European Union standards for potatoes (IFAD, 2014e). The farmers benefit from links to strong markets and the company is able to spread its risk and meet supermarket demand by having a good supply chain.

In Indonesia, a project that brings together IFAD funding and know-how from the Mars company is putting the cocoa industry back on its feet again (IFAD, 2013h). Most of the world's cocoa is produced by 6 million smallholder farmers, who cannot keep up with demand (World Cocoa Foundation, 2014). Through training in new techniques, farmers have been able to triple their yields (IFAD, 2013h).

In Guatemala, a producers' association (AGRESEM) bought irrigation equipment, built a new storage facility, and worked with private sector partners to bring their produce to new markets. Today, AGRESEM sells to some of the biggest retailers in the world, including Wal-Mart in the United States. This is a major success for smallholders – but it doesn't happen without investment, partnership, government commitment, and an enabling environment.

In São Tomé and Príncipe, the Participatory Smallholder Agriculture and Artisanal Fisheries Development Programme helped revive cocoa production and export. Nearly 2,000 producers belong to the Organic Cocoa Export Cooperative, and sell their cocoa to the international chocolate industry (Ledwith, 2012).

Policy

Smallholder organizations also give individual farmers a stronger voice in policy decisions that affect their livelihoods, and consequently, the lives of everyone else who depends on them for food. Every country needs policies for inclusive growth to maximize its food production potential. Those policies will have a major effect on whether we can feed the future. The views and experiences of smallholders must inform those decisions, and make sure they are sustainable, not short-sighted.

At the country level, IFAD helps government 'talk policy' with national stakeholders, especially farmer groups, cooperatives, and other rural people's organizations. IFAD also strengthens these community-based groups to play a more effective role in policy dialogue. Through this two-pronged process, policy design can draw on more relevant evidence and local experience (IFAD, Environment and Climate Division, 2015).

In the eastern region of El Salvador, for example, an IFAD-supported project is helping the government mainstream climate and environmental dimensions into business plans for smallholders, as well as bringing potential financing for adaptation initiatives. Among its activities, the project will generate weather forecasts for smallholders, including through mobile telephones and the internet. At the same time, the project will train organizations of women, youth, and indigenous peoples in skills such as public speaking and negotiation. This will empower them to participate more effectively in national policy processes related to rural development and climate change. The project will also set quotas for the participation of women and youth in value chain interventions, including in leadership. In this way, their voices will be heard (ibid.).

In 2009, IFAD launched a programme to strengthen farmers' organizations in African countries, as well as their regional and pan-African networks (IFAD, 2013i). In the pilot phase, which lasted to 2012, the programme supported 55 national organizations in 39 countries and their four regional networks in sub-Saharan Africa. Among its achievements, farmers' organizations developed more than 44 policy positions and attended local, national, and regional policy forums thereby improving their recognition, reputation, and credibility among governments, local authorities, and partners. They also launched the Pan-African Farmers' Organization (PAFO), the first continental organization of African farmers.

In its main phase, which runs until 2017, the programme continues to strengthen the institutional capacities of farmers' organizations, which includes giving them a greater say in agricultural policies and programmes. In addition, the main phase is helping organizations develop economic services that can support the integration of smallholder farmers in value chains. The inclusion of a fifth regional network has expanded the geographical area to the North Africa region. The programme now supports 68 national farmers' organizations in 49 countries and their five regional networks, as well as PAFO.

Of course, all these many factors I have enumerated do not necessarily follow from A–Z. The reality of inclusive community development is far from linear, and the need to be aware of so many issues at the same time creates a good deal of the challenge. We cannot wait for land tenure solutions before building microfinance institutions or strengthening the enabling policy environment.

There is, however, an underlying principle that must feed into everything we do to support smallholder farmers: profit and income are not dirty words for poor farmers. Whether the entrepreneur is a multinational firm or a young woman selling vegetables at a roadside stand, farming is a business. If farmers cannot make a profit to invest in their businesses, send their children to school, and buy the food they cannot grow, they have little incentive to stay in farming.

One thing has been clear to me for years: smallholder producers or rural people are not waiting for government handouts. All they want are economic opportunities, just like all businesses. What they want from government is an enabling environment with basic physical and social structures and infrastructure in order to thrive. I explore these issues at more length in Chapter 7.

Rural development doesn't come from a master plan – though without being strategic, we will not achieve universal eradication of poverty and hunger. But it is important to recognize that the goal and the people are inseparable. The impetus to achieve transformational development does not, ultimately, come from declarations and resolutions. It comes from local people who want, and deserve, the ability to provide for themselves and their families. Listening to them, and empowering them, makes for good business, and is also the main pathway to achieving the SDGs.

4.

Where are the farmers of tomorrow?

In Madagascar, Zoeliharimalala Nirinarisoa began processing yogurt, adding a medicinal crop called *moringa* to make her product more nutritious and give it a delicious flavour (IFAD Stories, 2016b). She then packaged and sold the product in the marketplace. Buoyed by her success, she began employing other community members.

This young woman's business is connected to PROSPERER, an IFAD-funded project in Madagascar that works with rural people in five of the country's poorest and most densely populated regions. Her story is a small illustration of how some young people are creating their own futures in rural communities, and how development projects can help to foster their success.

There is no Sustainable Development Goal (SDG) for youth or youth employment, though it is highlighted in Goal 8, Target 8.6: 'By 2020, substantially reduce the proportion of youth not in employment, education or training' (UN General Assembly, 2015b, 14). In fact, it is impossible to minimize the importance of this issue, and in particular the need to create decent, profitable employment for young people in rural areas.

A few statistics will serve to highlight why the issue of youth is so critical. Consider that in India, half of the population is under 25, which amounts to a staggering 625 million young women and men (Virmani, 2014). And by around 2020, some two-thirds of the population in the Near East and North Africa are expected to be under the age of 24. In sub-Saharan Africa alone, youth number 200 million, with an estimated 10 million per year entering the job market (African Development Bank et al., 2012). Agriculture and off-farm employment are going to be essential pathways to the future livelihoods of these young people, and can channel their energy and potential in ways that benefit food security, poverty reduction, and social and economic stability.

Granted, not every young person has the passion, drive, and entrepreneurial spirit to be a farmer. But we must encourage and empower those who do have these qualities to fulfil their dreams. And we must work harder to show sceptical youth how the definition of 'farming' is broader now than ever before.

Today's generation of young people – defined by the United Nations as those aged 15 to 24 – is the largest in history. In the developing world as a whole, they make up 25 per cent of the population (UN Population Fund, 2014).

Young people have power and persistence. Given the right conditions, a substantial young generation offers countries a priceless resource for economic development and social progress. In the current climate, however, many developed and developing countries – for many different reasons – are struggling to provide their young people with a future, either in cities or in rural areas.

Unfolding events in the Arab region to sub-Saharan Africa to Europe offer unsettling testimony to the consequences of neglecting development for populations that are young and unemployed. Although the level and nature of grievances differ, when young people are frustrated by poverty, lack of work, and lack of rights, they do not sit by passively. They will shape more than one country's future – not simply by what they do, but by the sheer force of their numbers.

This projected youth bulge is both a tremendous challenge and an unprecedented opportunity: if we can harness the power and creativity of young adults on every continent, we can address two major global challenges – population growth and urbanization – at the same time.

By 2050, world population is expected to surpass 9 billion. Meanwhile, more people are living in cities. Between 2010 and 2030, for instance, the share of Africans living in urban areas is projected to grow from 36 per cent to 50 per cent (African Development Bank Group, 2012). FAO estimates that, with no reduction of food losses and waste and no shift to more sustainable diets, food production will have to increase by 60 per cent to meet demand (FAO, 2012c). Yet the average age of farmers is about 60 years old, and the next generation is drawn increasingly to the promise of the city (FAO, 2014). Who will work the farms to feed the world?

The solutions to feeding a burgeoning world population, fighting poverty and hunger, reducing the pressure on our cities, and meeting the demands of youth for greater opportunity all hinge on addressing development in rural areas. We must create an environment that encourages young women and men to remain in their communities – one that allows them to find decent work, build prosperity, and pursue their dreams as Zoeliharimalala Nirinarisoa has done.

In Chapter 3, I argued that farming, on any scale, is a business. Thankfully, I am no longer alone in promoting the economic viability of smallholder farmers and their importance for food security and development. More and more policymakers and government leaders are calling for greater attention to the smallholder sector. But, ironically, the most sceptical audience of all may be the very one for whom farming holds out so much potential, and whom we so much need to choose agriculture as a profession: youth in developing countries.

The problem is not just about the lure of the city. Rural and urban areas are increasingly connected; high technology has great potential to reduce the remoteness of rural areas. But youth, along with other marginalized groups, are often unable to take advantage of the opportunities. Many youth who want to farm have no financial resources or collateral to kick-start their businesses. They may also lack access to modern communications technologies that would provide much-needed information, such as timely updates on weather and market conditions. And for these, and other reasons, they may not see themselves as potential farmers.

Yet the young generation of today has repeatedly shown that, given the right conditions, it can move mountains. Young people have embraced new media and have used it to make their voices heard. But are we listening to what they're telling us? We need a new generation to produce, process, and market the food that will feed the world. We need young people to play their part – as entrepreneurs, service providers, and wage earners – in the development and economic growth of their communities. Rural areas are key to providing opportunities for these energetic young people to contribute to society and to the big battles humanity faces today – against hunger, poverty, environmental degradation, and climate change. We need youth with convictions and determination to fight for good governance and social progress. Youth who can build their communities and challenge their leaders constructively. And leaders need to recognize that the younger generation is the future of any nation.

But in many developing countries, youth are abandoning life on the farm for the lure of the city. The decision to leave what they have always known, however, may be less an act of desire than of desperation.

At the very least, countries must not put systemic roadblocks in the path of those willing to work hard to earn a better life. And they must not allow conditions to persist that drive them away from everything they've known in order to survive.

When young rural women and men in developing countries cannot get an adequate education or make a living at home, they move to sprawling urban areas or to foreign countries they believe offer more hope. Some make good and continue to contribute to their communities by sending money home. Too many, however, become mired in urban poverty. This is a tremendous loss of human potential for themselves, their families, and their countries.

The key to meeting the world's future food needs – and to fighting the hunger and poverty that are concentrated in rural areas – is to create an environment that will encourage and enable young women and men to remain in their communities. They need opportunities to improve their own lives, obtain decent work, and pursue prosperity. There is no reason that rural areas cannot provide these opportunities, and in fact, we must make it possible for them to do so. Urban areas have a finite capacity to absorb youth migration – we need a healthy urban–rural balance for a sustainable future.

What do youth need most?

Basic education is essential to poverty reduction. Yet still today, in many countries, one young person in four is illiterate – and most are women (UNESCO Institute for Statistics, 2016). The proportion of young people with basic education deficits is greater in rural than in urban areas, which is not surprising given that rural areas are disadvantaged in numerous other sectors as well.

Even youth who receive a solid education in the fundamentals, however, may not be well-equipped for the labour market. In the Near East and North Africa, some governments have made significant investments in education, but the system is not delivering a workforce that meets employers' demands. As a result, in some countries more than half of graduates do not find jobs. In North Africa, the youth unemployment rate is 30 per cent. Across the continent, according to a recent report, youth account for 60 per cent of all African unemployed (African Development Bank Group et al., 2012).

Apart from education, young people also need vocational training and apprenticeships to give them the relevant knowledge and skills to find work or create jobs for themselves. Targeted training programmes can help youth transition to the job market, while helping countries meet specific labour needs. Below, I provide some examples of IFAD's work in this area across Africa.

In Madagascar, rural transformation holds out the promise of providing a variety of jobs, including off-farm employment, but youth need the skills to seize emerging opportunities. To that end, IFAD is supporting the National Strategy for Agricultural and Rural Training with a vocational training programme that targets vulnerable groups, including uneducated youth (IFAD Operations, n.d. e). The programme works with IFAD-supported projects to identify and train young farmers, agricultural technicians, and extension agents in all 13 regions. It matches young women and men to businesses of all kinds – from learning how to make pottery and weave clothes to obtaining practical experience in shops and on farms. Thousands of young rural workers have the chance to learn skills through apprenticeships, which is helping build a stable, skilled workforce for Malagasy small businesses.

In several West and Central African nations, IFAD provided training and business development services for young women and men involved in farming and other rural enterprises. With help from their mentors, these agricultural entrepreneurs – or *agripreneurs* – are starting up new ventures across the value chain. They demonstrate that agriculture is an exciting, modern profession through which young people can contribute financially to their communities as both producers and consumers (IFAD, 2015g).

In Benin, lack of access to markets and microfinance contributes to the growth of poverty, including among uneducated and unemployed youth (Rural Poverty Portal, n.d. e). IFAD supported the establishment and growth of financial service associations – owned by rural people – that offer credit and savings products to more than 83,000 clients through some 190 village banks. By 2011, these associations had extended nearly half of all their available credit to young women and men who use loans in different ways – from starting up taxi-bike companies and shoe shops to buying improved seeds and other inputs to improve farm productivity.

Too often, however, banks refuse credit to potential farmers because of their youth, or because they don't see farming as a viable business, or because the farmers do not have sufficient collateral. Under these circumstances, how can we expect farming to attract youth? Access to credit and financial services is critical for both agricultural and off-farm employment for youth.

In 2011, IFAD set up the Global Youth Innovation Network (GYIN) with key youth partners as a learning platform that connects young entrepreneurs. Five years later, IFAD, GYIN, and the Government of Senegal teamed up for a youth conference that gave African women and men in rural areas the opportunity to discuss key issues and learn new skills (IFAD Stories, 2016). At the conference, rural youth reported that lack of credit, poor access to information, and negative perceptions around farming are the leading reasons why African young people are leaving small farming at such alarming rates. Many youth view farming as the work of the past, not the future.

Thankfully, there are many exceptions. Just as PROSPERER gave Zoeliharimalala Nirinarisoa the tools to start her yogurt business in Madagascar, the Rural Finance Institution Building Programme (RFIN) gave Nurat Okeowo an opportunity to pursue her dreams in Nigeria. When young women like Okeowo – who lacks a high school diploma – approach financial institutions in my home country, they are often turned away. Unfortunately, when lenders calculate risk, the drive and passion of an applicant may not weigh as heavily in the balance as the perceived undependability of smallholders. Through the RFIN programme, however, Nurat received a loan and training to manage a fish farm. Since then, she has expanded her business significantly, and hired employees (ibid.). In North Africa, where 29 per cent of youth are unemployed, the Rural Youth Economic Empowerment Program (RYEEP) is increasing financial services for young people in Egypt, Yemen, Morocco, and Tunisia (Making Cents, n.d.). RYEEP also provides youth with non-financial services such as job training, job market information, financial literacy courses, entrepreneurship classes, and, in some cases, jobs. To date, these types of services have been shown to be more important as a motivating force for youth than the financial services themselves. By 2016, five RYEEP pilot projects are expected to have helped more than 3,750 youth find work in the formal sector or create their own jobs.

In our globalized world, access to information is power, and it flows two ways. Farmers need to receive better information about markets, weather, and opportunities to enhance and expand their businesses. But they also need to reach out to potential consumers who, today, may live far beyond the borders of their villages.

The Global Youth Innovative Network in Senegal is showing how information and communications technologies (ICTs) can be used to transform the lives of rural African women who work in agriculture (Global Youth Innovation Network, n.d.). One young woman, Awa Caba, took part in the IFAD-sponsored Agricultural Value Chains Support Project, an initiative better known as PAFA, its French acronym. After discovering the need to improve the price and market information put in place by PAFA, she was later hired as a consultant to the project (IFAD Stories, 2016).

With support from IFAD and other donors, Caba also co-founded an e-commerce site called *Sooretul* (based on a Wolof word that means 'No longer far away'). On the one hand, the site helps consumers find local food products not available in large shopping centres. On the other, it enables women working in the agro-food industry to showcase their 'made in Senegal' products both within the country and abroad (Sooretul, n.d.). In this way, it bridges the gap between urban consumers and rural producers.

The boundaries between rural and urban areas are not nearly as clear cut as they once were. Research funded by IFAD points to marked changes in the nature of food consumption and production (Tacoli, 2015). This, too, offers many opportunities for youth, if they have the education, tools, and ambition to succeed.

Traditionally, farmers in rural areas produced food primarily for urban areas. City dwellers, faced with an abundance, often purchased more than they needed, much of which went to waste. Meanwhile, the poorest rural smallholders – the ones who had grown this precious food that was being wasted – often went to bed hungry.

Today, the dynamics are shifting profoundly. Many people in rural areas are buying more of their food instead of growing it. In Vietnam, for example, 55 per cent of rural households are net rice buyers, and 22 per cent do not have access to productive land (ibid.). Meanwhile, high levels of unemployment and underemployment in urban areas mean that many city dwellers suffer from food insecurity or cannot afford to buy nutritious food.

This is a message that must get out to our youth. Too many young people believe that city life offers a fast track to jobs and prosperity. Once there, however, they may join the ranks of the urban poor who do not eat well or enough.

Researchers have begun to understand 'rural' and 'urban' as a continuum. In between the two extremes of 'city' and 'village' are market towns and large villages, which play a critical role in transforming food systems. These 'rural cities' provide local producers with more outlets to sell their goods, better access to information, and opportunities for off-farm jobs – everything from traditional agricultural processing and distribution to preparing goods and services that cater to urban customers.

As I discuss further in Chapter 10, the implications of blurring boundaries between 'urban' and 'rural' are complex. At the very least, however, the shifting landscape offers new opportunities for youth in agriculture. Those who do not choose to work directly on the land as farmers could well build a future in a more urban environment that supports rural transformation.

Policymakers must start to recognize the crucial interdependence between urbanization and rural development. Urban and rural areas cannot be seen in isolation from each other. In fact, no country has successfully industrialized without first greatly increasing the productivity of its agriculture sector. We have seen over recent decades what happened to countries with mineral and energy resources that neglected agriculture. Their cities grew and so did GDP – but often so did conflict, and so did food import bills. Where are the youth of these countries now? Failing to provide opportunities for youth to reach their potential undermines food security, weakens the social fabric of nations, and exacerbates migration and instability.

It will also undermine the SDGs. Smallholder agriculture is particularly vital to achieving SDGs 1 and 2. For us to achieve those goals, farming must be seen as an attractive, lucrative, and dignified profession for youth. It requires a range of investments to revitalize rural areas and give youth the hope they so desperately need.

Challenges facing youth

Even when all other conditions empower youth, the unexpected can scuttle the most carefully prepared plans. This is true personally – as when the war in Biafra changed my own life – and nationally. I was one of the lucky ones. The very day I decided to join the Biafran army was the day my hometown was overrun by the federal army. My family escaped into the bush that night, and I escaped what would have been a wasted life. How many countries have made hard-won development gains, only to see them undone, rolled back, or destroyed by conflict?

As I argued in Chapter 2, agricultural development and peacebuilding can go hand in hand. Farming may not plant the seeds for peace, but it can fertilize them. And in the process of building food security, we can strengthen overall security by building community. Particular notice needs to be given to the engagement of youth in this process, which is paramount to ward off disaffected youth from channelling their frustration into extremist activities.

Wars are mainly fought by young people. When conflict ends, they often find themselves destitute and without options. IFAD has supported agricultural and rural development projects that gave these young people, returnees, and other survivors of conflict the prospect of a productive livelihood.

In Nigeria, the Niger Delta is better known for its violence than for its farming. For many years, it was considered a 'no-go zone'. But for several years, an IFAD-funded project has been creating a new generation of rural entrepreneurs (IFAD Operations, n.d. b). These are young people, many of them university graduates, who have learned that fish farming and vegetable growing can be lucrative businesses. They are contributing to the stability, wealth, and nutrition of their communities. More than that, by taking responsibility for their garden plots and fish farms, the young farmers enjoy a sense of belonging.

In Egypt, an IFAD-supported project has enabled unemployed graduates to turn desert into farmland, thereby growing communities as well as food. The Egyptian Government identified the need for more arable farmland to help feed its growing population, and began providing disadvantaged Egyptians loans to buy land in the desert as long as they agreed to farm it. Communities have taken root, schools have opened, and links have been made with major markets domestically and internationally.

Opportunity flowering in the desert – it sounds like a miracle but it isn't, actually. It is a strategy, a partnership, and an example of people-centred investment that works.

In Sierra Leone, the civil war between 1991 and 2002 hit the districts of Kono and Kailahun the hardest. Building on its previous experience in the country, IFAD developed a project that would allow the community to play a leading role in restoring the devastated agricultural sector. The Rehabilitation and Community-Based Poverty Reduction Project sought to absorb an estimated 20,000 ex-combatants with a farming background – half of whom were youth – into the country's agricultural sector (IFAD, 2013a). The project provided youth with funds to lease or purchase agricultural land, farm inputs, grain stores, rice mills, and drying floors, as well as food processing and storage equipment.

For all the foreign aid from donors, all the incentives of national governments, all the investments of agencies like IFAD, all the remittances sent home to support farmers – it is up to young people themselves to take charge of their futures. With unemployment and underemployment standing at around 30 per cent among Africa's 200 million youth, young people cannot just wait for governments to create jobs. They must do it themselves.

To return to the central parable of this book: when you go to the stream to fetch water, your bucket will be filled with the water that is yours. No one can take the water that is meant for you, but first you must walk to the stream, bend down and dip your bucket. So I would like to issue this challenge to Africa's young men and women: do not sit at home waiting for the government or your parents, uncles or aunts to find you work or pay your way. When you see an opportunity, take it.

Walking to the stream is not always easy. I was not born into a wealthy family, and my own education was interrupted by the

Biafran War. There were times when I thought I would never reach the stream. But I did, and I can assure you my bucket is not empty.

I have confidence that if we do our part in helping the younger generation reach the stream, they will repay us by rejuvenating Africa's agricultural sector and helping Africa take its place as a leader in the developing and developed world.

Youth are Africa's future

Let me end with a closer look at the potential for youth in Africa, my home.

When I envision the future of Africa, I picture a continent where 200 million young people channel their energy and creativity into building new and exciting businesses; a continent where small- and medium-sized businesses provide employment and contribute to a strong economic base for societies; a continent of endless possibility that has vanquished poverty and hunger.

Africa holds tremendous opportunity for entrepreneurs. Consumer spending is expected to reach US$1 tn – and by some estimates US$1.4 tn – by 2020 (Munang and Mgendi, 2015). And the population is expected to keep growing, reaching 1.34 billion by 2020, and doubling by 2050, with the largest labour pool of young people in the world.

Which sectors hold out the most promise for youth?

Africa is rich in minerals and other natural resources. Sub-Saharan Africa produces 77 per cent of the world's platinum metals; 60 per cent of its cobalt (used for batteries and metal alloys); 46 per cent of its natural industrial diamonds; and an abundance of gold, uranium, oil, and gas (US Geological Survey, 2016).

But my vision for Africa's future is not built on a foundation of extractive industries. These riches have not translated into wide-ranging job creation, or social welfare and stability. They have not fed hungry people. They have not reduced poverty.

On the contrary, strong evidence suggests that poor countries with rich natural resources grow two to three times more *slowly* than countries without these resources (Auty, 2001). While a relatively small number of people have become incredibly rich from Africa's vast mineral resources, poverty remains endemic. An estimated 43 per cent of Africans live in extreme poverty. This adds up to more than 330 million children, women, and men (Beegle et al., 2016).

The 'resource curse' continues to plague many countries in Africa, impeding inclusive growth. Until the continent is better able to address ongoing governance challenges, owning these resources may not actually be a long-term blessing.

We know that income inequality can lead to slower or less sustainable economic growth – a fact reported by the International Monetary Fund (Dabla-Norris et al., 2015). So when Africa looks at economic growth, it needs to consider ways that also promote greater income equality.

Over the years, I have often asked myself why Africa lags behind other economies.

Lack of industry is certainly a factor. According to the Brookings Institution, manufacturing output per person in sub-Saharan Africa is about a-third of the developing country average. And manufactured exports per person are about 10 per cent of the average for low-income countries (Page, 2014).

Colonialism also casts a long shadow. Perhaps because of that legacy, several African countries have been plagued by inadequate governance, political and civil unrest, immature institutions, corruption, and lack of transparency. These block progress at all levels, from the social to the economic.

Lack of infrastructure across the continent also impedes growth. Roads are often poorly maintained or non-existent. If smallholder farmers live many hours from the nearest market town, this leaves them with no real chance to participate in the economy and no real chance of improving their condition by investing in their businesses.

In addition to infrastructure there is the issue of energy. The energy supply in sub-Saharan Africa is so meagre that 621 million Africans do not have access to electricity at all (Africa Progress Panel, 2015). To make matters worse, poor Africans who are not on the grid pay US$10 per kWh of energy, compared with Americans, who pay only 12 cents (ibid.).

Does all of this mean that smallholder agriculture is non-viable? Or that the conventional view of the small farm as primitive and a thing of the past is actually true? By no means. These barriers can and must be overcome – every developed country overcame them at some stage and increased the productivity of their agriculture sector. It may be challenging, but it remains true that the best way for Africa to grow its economy is through agriculture and rural transformation.

The opportunities agriculture presents are more than simply growing food. In its broadest sense, agriculture covers every step of the value chain – from primary production to eventual consumption, both on-farm and off-farm. Along the way, the need for storage, conservation, packaging, marketing, information technology, and transport present myriad opportunities for employment, especially among youth. Investing in agriculture does not only benefit farmers; it benefits the entire community.

There are powerful arguments for creating vibrant rural economies in Africa. Africa is urbanizing rapidly. And rural people will continue to migrate to urban areas in search of better lives and livelihoods as long as African agriculture remains at the subsistence level, as long as the roads are unpaved, and villages have no electricity, health clinics, or clean water.

Yet rapid urbanization comes with its problems, including overcrowding, pollution, and disease. In fact, evidence shows that what is described as 'rapid urbanization' is actually bulging urban slums which are expanding due to rural–urban migration (UN-Habitat, 2006). Between 2002 and 2007, 60 per cent of urban residents in developing countries were victims of crime (UN-Habitat, 2007). In Africa, urbanization has mainly resulted in higher levels of poverty and inequality (African Development Bank Group, 2012).

By investing in rural economies, we can create a range of opportunities for young people in rural areas – in Africa, surely, but also elsewhere – so they are not compelled to migrate to urban centres and big cities or abroad, where they often face an uncertain future (IFAD, 2014f). Investing in young rural people is a simple and elegant solution to some of our most pressing problems. It is not a complete solution, of course, but it is essential. It is also a generational, national, and international priority. The dividends are many. It helps eliminate poverty and hunger. It curtails migration to cities and abroad. And it lays a solid foundation for national, regional, and global security.

Both rural and urban youth need honest role models to mentor, support, encourage, and inspire them – not political rhetoric and corrupt officials and business 'gurus' – to show them the way to honest wealth creation by the work of their hands, the intelligence of their minds, and the belief in the goodness and integrity of their character.

We need to make a career in farming as appealing as a career in high-tech, and more secure than the uncertain and often dangerous prospects of life in the city. Globally, rising demand for food has created enormous opportunities, and – with the help of research, technology, and modern markets – developing country agriculture can be a viable business and remunerative profession for the young. We can create the conditions for tomorrow's food producers to thrive, or we can allow the huge potential of the younger generation to be frustrated or to drain away. The latter course is not really an option, however, as it would put a question mark over not only our food security but our collective future.

5.

Moving closer to gender equality

It has often been observed that women are increasingly the farmers of the developing world (Slavchecska et al., 2016). People speak of the 'feminization' of agriculture. But when we talk about gender we need to remember that it is not just a women's issue. It is an issue for women and men, a dimension that needs to be factored into all development activity.

In my career as a researcher, we often started working with women first. But we also learned, quite quickly, that we could not limit our work to women. For change to take hold in a community, men must also participate. When men see benefits flowing into the family and the community, resistance often falls away. Women and men alike take ownership, and a project becomes more sustainable.

Investing in a man may build his capacity, but investing in a woman builds a community. Longstanding evidence suggests that women are more likely than men to spend money they earn on food for the family. Too often, however, in rural societies, women are second-class citizens without rights to the land they farm, without the same access to credit and equipment as men, and without authority in their homes or communities. This results in higher rates of poverty for themselves and their families. In Cote d'Ivoire, for example, a US$10 increase in women's income brought the same level of improvement in child health and nutrition as a US$110 increase in men's income (Hoddinott and Haddad, 1995).

In another case, I once helped develop varieties of rice that grow upright. The men liked them because they were robust. But it turned out the women farmers didn't like them, and this created a problem. Since the new variety grew upright, it did not cover the surface of the ground, and this made it easier for weeds to grow. As women were responsible for weeding, it increased their already huge workload. We also found that women also preferred softer rice varieties because they were the ones who had to pound the rice to separate the grain from the outer husk.

This example shows that agricultural science may develop a new variety of seed, but it needs the social sciences to understand how that seed will be used in the world outside the laboratory. People don't live in laboratories; they live in a social and environmental reality, a context, which we need to keep in view. The context in which rural women live and work is often harsh. Extreme gender inequalities persist in many parts of the developing world, especially in rural areas. Rural women and girls juggle many roles and responsibilities. Apart from farming, they raise children, care for the elderly, prepare food, gather firewood and water, and undertake all the other countless, unheralded tasks that keep a family functioning. In developing countries in Africa, Asia, and the Pacific, women typically work 12 hours per week more than men. Yet their contributions are often unrecognized and unpaid (IFAD, 2012b).

There are so many aspects to women's inequality that hold them back: lack of education, unequal workloads and property rights, limited control over resources, and limited participation in the decisions that affect their lives, to name only a few (ibid.).

These factors may never be voiced aloud, and yet they must surely affect a family's well-being. What incentive does a woman have to increase productivity when it only means extra work without a share in the financial gains? Yet when conditions become more equitable, women are more engaged, productivity increases, and the whole family benefits. In fact, a recent McKinsey Global Institute report found that advancing gender equality in the workplace could add US$12 tn to global GDP by 2025 (Woetzel et al., 2015).

Closing the gender gap, then, concerns everyone. It is not enough for interventions to 'include' women: they must empower women – economically, socially, and politically. Poor rural women deserve more money, more status, and more decision-making power both in the affairs of the home and in the community. With these in hand, they can drive sustainable, transformational change.

What would the world look like if we closed the gender gap?

Women and men would have equal access to opportunities and services. They would exert equal control over resources. And they would have an equal say in decisions at all levels. Based on all evidence to date, this would lead to higher economic growth and a better quality of life for all. Knowing how to work together and respecting the individuality of each gender foster greater community cohesion and coherence.

Women now make up more than 40 per cent of the global labour force, but their numbers are even greater – more than 43 per cent – in agriculture as a whole. Within the livestock sector, the numbers are higher again – about 70 per cent of those employed (World Bank, 2012). Livestock is a crucial source of income for poor rural women, with two thirds of poor livestock owners, some 400 million people, being women (FAO, 2016).

According to FAO, if women had equal access to productive inputs, such as improved seeds and fertilizers, their yields would increase by 20 to 30 per cent. This would boost total agricultural output by up to 4 per cent in developing countries, reducing the number of hungry people globally by 12 to 17 per cent, or 100 million to 150 million people (FAO, 2011b).

Sometimes, we cannot imagine what changes will transpire from the most basic infrastructure. In Morocco, I visited an IFAD-supported project that helped finance a 3-kilometre feeder road. The road was intended to reduce transportation costs, but it did so much more.

A group of women from the village of Ouaouisseft told me the road was helping them save hours of time in transporting water. With this precious additional time, they invested in growing and selling herbs and medicinal plants. They even started a childcare facility in their village so they could earn more money without neglecting their children. Sometimes, as I discuss in Chapter 8, small and simple are best.

The 2030 Agenda rightly recognizes the critical role played by women. But while Sustainable Development Goal (SDG) 5 targets gender equality, all development – including agricultural and rural development – needs to embed this goal in its interventions to reach other objectives across the board.

That does not mean there is a simple, one-size-fits-all approach. Gender inequalities are complex, and difficult to untangle. Where to begin? As a start, we could recognize the difference between hunger and poverty, and how they affect women and men differently.

Hunger and poverty are not the same but influence each other. Poverty causes hunger because poor people cannot afford to buy the food they need. The resulting food insecurity and malnutrition damage their long-term health and that of their children, thus critically reducing people's physical ability to work and fulfil their potential – keeping generations truly trapped in poverty.

Among the causes of poverty and hunger, one could cite disparities based on location, ethnicity, disability, age, and gender. Indeed, despite the lack of sex-disaggregated statistics, we know beyond doubt that hunger and poverty disproportionately affect women and girls. In 2015, a UN Women's flagship report noted that women work two and a half times longer than men every day on unpaid care work, principally with children and elderly people (UN Women, 2015). This has a massive impact on their capacity to earn money, educate themselves, enjoy free time, and interact with others outside the home.

Many innovative tools are emerging to save women time, reduce the drudgery of their work, and increase productivity across their entire labour profile. The 2014 IFAD Sharefair on Rural Women's Technologies, for example, exhibited nearly 100 labour-saving innovations from 14 countries in East and Southern Africa (Tole, 2014). These included technologies for agriculture and livestock, value addition and income generation, and information management and household use.

In the developing world, fetching fuel and water is one of the most onerous of tasks, and carried out mostly by women and girls. An IFAD-supported project in Kenya made better access to water and health services a starting point for improving the well-being of women and their dependents. Overall, the project built 26 shallow wells to serve 32,000 people, as well as 17 new piped schemes. In addition, it developed 20 springs and built 24 rain water tanks for primary schools (IFAD, 2012b).

Elizabeth Wanjiru, from the Kiambu District of central Kenya, used to spend as many as six hours a day fetching water for her family. The nearest spring was two kilometres away; queues were long and the water was filled with sediment. Without clean water, hygiene and disease risks increase. By the project's end, with the communal water point about 30 metres from home, Elizabeth was spending just two minutes fetching clean water.

Think of the impact of gaining six hours every day. In Elizabeth's village, some women chose to plant and tend kitchen gardens or start profitable small enterprises. They took part in women's groups organized by the project, where they learned about better livestock breeds and crop species; how to prevent soil erosion and harvest rainwater; and new skills such as beekeeping and aquaculture (ibid.).

In 2015, IFAD studied the impact of its investments in seven water projects, looking at access to water, the time saved by households, their use of that time, and the workloads of household members. Before the projects were introduced, women were spending on average 3.5 hours a day collecting water; after the water investments, the labour for this task had dropped to an average of 1.5 hours (IFAD, Policy and Technical Advisory Division, 2016b).

Women and girls may be spending less time fetching and carrying water, but the improvements have not changed the essential fact: they still do most of the labour. It's time for this to change. According to the study, the multiple positive impacts of water investments support the drive for equitable workloads between men and women (ibid.).

Gender and climate change

Since girls and women remain the primary collectors of fuel and water in most developing countries, they are on the front lines of climate change. If water sources dry up due to higher temperatures, for example, girls and women will be the first affected. In most countries reliant on rain-fed agriculture and natural resources, poor rural women have fewer assets and less decision-making power than men, and are even more exposed to the impact of climate change. In Chapter 6, I reflect on the relationship between climate change and agriculture, but here I focus on how women can play a pivotal role in community-based adaptation.

Water scarcity is one of the greatest challenges faced by communities in the Lubombo region of Swaziland. People – usually women – commonly walk long distances to fetch drinking water, and sometimes share water sources with livestock. Not only does this practice mean that women spend a lot of time fetching water, it also poses significant health risks for their families.

But the women of the Vikizijula Chiefdom in Lubombo gave life to the saying that 'if spiders' webs can unite, they can tie up a lion'. For one month, as part of an IFAD-supported project, women of all ages came together in the chiefdom and built water harvesting tanks to provide potable water for their families. The project aims to reduce land degradation, preserve biodiversity, and mitigate the impact of climate change through the application of sustainable land management practices – including water conservation, conservation agriculture, rangeland management, forestation, and increased capacity for biomass energy production. It has trained women in the practical skills required to construct water harvesting tanks for their own households. This is a lifelong skill that some are now using to supplement their household income by building tanks for others (ibid.).

Land tenure, an issue that I discussed in Chapter 3, also has a strong relationship both to gender equality and climate change. Generally, when people have more secure tenure, they are more likely to invest in their land, plant trees, and use environmentally sustainable agricultural methods. Tenure security for women in particular can also allow them to use land as collateral for loans, which contributes substantially to their empowerment (Rural Poverty Portal, 2013).

As I mentioned earlier, an IFAD-supported initiative in Ethiopia issued land certificates to all women-headed households in the target area. In married households, women and men were registered as co-owners. Now that they own the land, women are planting perennials and trees, and using soil and water conservation methods to increase the productivity of the plots. This is helping them adapt to climate change, while increasing their income. This allows them to buy more food and to raise poultry and cattle, which in turn helps to increase and diversify their family's diet, leading to higher food security (Rural Poverty Portal, 2012).

Being respected and having a voice in the community is often linked to owning assets. As women now are landholders, they are joining elders' and land administration committees or are functioning as arbitrators in land disputes. All of these positive changes have increased women's self-confidence, empowered them on many levels, and enabled them to serve their communities.

The long march to a distant well can be measured by time and distance, and land tenure can be determined by the name on a certificate. But there are clearly other less tangible barriers that prevent women from enjoying equal status with men. Practices and mindsets can form invisible walls that block women's access to services, knowledge, and opportunity.

For example, education is obviously key to women's empowerment, but training options are sometimes just distant dreams and aspirations for poor rural women. A group of eight courageous young Yemeni women seized the opportunity to train as veterinary professionals with support from an IFAD-funded project. The first two graduates became a source of inspiration and knowledge for their communities. Meanwhile, the excellence of all the students eventually inspired the institute to open admissions to women without discrimination (IFAD, 2012b).

Women as agents of change

Since 2015, Yemen has been in the grips of a civil war, creating a daunting humanitarian crisis. UN Women reported that women in Yemen are disproportionately affected due to restrictions of mobility, decision-making power, and lack of access and control over resources. They also have poor access to information, whether about their human rights or matters of basic hygiene (Inter-Agency Standing Committee, 2015).

In the face of conflict, women can clearly experience additional social, economic, and political constraints. But even in a seemingly stable environment, women can also be at a disadvantage compared to men. Emerging evidence suggests that where women live in the developing world can affect the quality of their lives. If she lives in a territory with dynamic markets, productive economic sectors, and public policies that target women's integration into the economy, she stands a greater chance at economic equality. If she doesn't have these geographic advantages, she will not be the only one to suffer: the economic inequalities affecting women also undermine the development of a country. In 2016, research funded by IFAD and Canada's International Development Research Centre (IDRC) showed that where a woman lives in Latin America affects her capacity to enjoy economic equality with men (RIMISP, 2016).

For poor rural producers in developing countries around the world, distance and disconnection from functioning markets are a huge challenge, for both women and men. But women are often more disadvantaged because they may lack literacy or numeracy skills. They may also have trouble securing credit to start businesses.

Intervening in such a situation, where there are both material and social barriers to women's advancement, as well as skill and knowledge gaps, can be complex. It is important to design strategies that address the complexity of issues in a sustained way over time, and also engage the community.

One example of this is the development of the Puno-Cusco Corridor Project (CORREDOR) in Peru, which found innovative ways to foster new enterprises and stimulate the local economy (IFAD, n.d. c). In so doing, women have learned how to obtain what they need to forge their own development. This project undertook this ambitious goal in a remote and mountainous area of the Peruvian Andes where poverty was entrenched, leaving few opportunities, especially for women. And yet even here, community-driven development has paid off, demonstrating its ability to deliver results in varied contexts.

As a first step, the project encouraged poor rural women to keep better track of their money. Some 7,400 women opened savings accounts, more than tripling the project's initial target (ibid.). This went hand-in-hand with a microcredit programme because demand for savings accounts increased when borrowers saw it gave them access to credit and provided a family safety net. Women were able to make investments that met the specific needs of their families, whether that was better education and health, or starting up a business. Apart from the savings and credit programmes, the project also offered training to prepare business plans – skills that allowed women to increase their income by more than 20 per cent (IFAD, n.d. a).

The project is just one example of how IFAD supports women as agents of change in their communities. We work with them to defend their land rights, improve access to water, education, training, and credit – and strengthen their leadership roles. Sometimes it's not simply a question of providing women with more financial autonomy; they may also need a space outside the company of men to share experiences with their peers and pursue collective strategies that enhance their status in the community. This was the case in our work with young indigenous women in India.

All youth are hindered by lack of access to land, markets, finance, education, and training, but young women, especially in rural areas, are held back still further by cultural and social norms. As a result, they are even less likely than boys to finish school and more likely to marry early (UNICEF, n.d.). Along with this comes the added risk of multiple births, ill health, and gender-based violence. Young indigenous rural women are perhaps the most marginalized of all.

Working with adolescent girls and young women presents a unique opportunity to transform lives – not only their own, but also those of the generations that follow. We must listen to the voices of women who have been excluded or marginalized by race, age, caste, or disability – those whose stories are harder to hear and whose problems are harder to solve.

In India, IFAD works in Odisha State, which has one of the highest numbers of particularly vulnerable indigenous groups in the country. A tribal empowerment and livelihoods programme supported by IFAD set up self-help groups for women, and involved tribal groups in the planning and implementation of various development initiatives, in particular the development of natural resources. Belonging to a self-help group gave the women more confidence, knowing they had strength in numbers. In small groups, they knocked on every door in the village to speak about how rampant alcohol abuse was the prime cause of domestic violence. Social change takes time, but the women report that men are gradually changing their behaviour (IFAD, India Country Office, 2011).

This change in the social context and relations in the village incited further actions, but this time in the economic realm. Women in the group branched out into income-generating activities, producing tamarind – the sweet and sour pulp so popular in India. Eventually, they started selling tamarind as a collective to cut out the intermediaries who were taking a large slice of the profits. With their earnings, they bought a tamarind press machine – a huge improvement over processing pulp by hand that saved them two hours of work a day. It also made the remaining work much easier (IFAD, 2012b).

In Baunsipada, another remote village, a self-help group began an entrepreneurial activity that had economic as well as health and safety benefits. Women from the Bonda tribe learned to assemble solar LED lanterns for sale through their self-help group. Just one month after they received their first training, the group was receiving orders from schools and other institutions in the district. The solar lanterns replace kerosene lamps, which are costly and dangerous (ibid.).

Women-only groups are one kind of solution, for some contexts. IFAD also supports producer groups with both female and male participants, in line with encouraging inclusiveness and participatory approaches. Because if in a community women are disadvantaged and poor because of their gender, it is not just a woman's issue, but rather an issue for the whole community.

The results from three IFAD-supported projects I visited in Ethiopia are also instructive. They show the positive results from women and men working together. And they show what happens when they don't.

Two projects had explicitly responded to the local social dynamic, and were participatory and inclusive. The farmers, both women and men, had formed strong organizations. They were financing their business through rural savings and credit organizations, and irrigating their crops through a community-based water users' association. Yields, incomes, and nutrition had all improved.

At the third project, participants did not address social issues. Without farmers' organizations, men dominated discussions and excluded women. These farmers saw no real improvements in yields, income, or nutrition. They could not even get to the basic step of boxing their produce for market.

Gender is a cross-cutting issue, which is why IFAD is mainstreaming the gender dimension into all its programmes and projects. In Guatemala, for example, IFAD supported a project involving both indigenous women and men weavers. It connected them to profitable overseas markets with support from IFAD and practical guidance from *Asociación Guatemalteca de Exportadores* (AGEXPORT), the Guatemalan exporters' association. AGEXPORT helped one group of women weavers by advising them to blend traditional colours and techniques with modern designs to enhance their appeal. The group also received other critical elements for their success, including support for business training and loans to upgrade their looms. The women and men weavers involved in the new venture earned up to 90 per cent more than when they sold their textiles only on local markets (ibid.).

As a multi-faceted issue rather than a single theme or sector, gender involves numerous aspects of the social and economic fabric of communities. This is why it requires a sustained approach over time to reap the full benefits of development in an inclusive manner. In 2012, in the village of Minkoa in Cameroon, I met a group of women who had planted improved varieties of cassava, and enhanced their production and productivity. With increased income, the women were able to feed and clothe their families better and send their children to school on a full stomach. But empowerment and development can go further and do more. One of the women, Susanna Nke, gave me a message for policymakers on behalf of the village committee: 'The rural women of our villages must really reach full autonomy. The arduous nature of their work must be reduced. We want to move from the hoe to the tractor. To transform our lives, we need modern equipment, water, electricity, telephone ... and why not internet?' (Nwanze, 2012b).

This is a vision of rural transformation, a deep, lasting, and comprehensive revitalization. As we work toward achieving the 2030 Agenda, we need to understand Nke's message and what it really means. Can the 'full autonomy' that she and others in her village want, and the tools to transform their lives, be delivered by development activities? Yes – as long as we recognize that they, the participants in these projects, will be doing the transforming.

Household methodologies

In the spirit of people-centred development that gives full space to both genders, IFAD has been pioneering a simple, but powerful, approach known as 'household methodologies' (IFAD, 2014b). Too often, development activities stay focused at the village level. The household methodologies approach brings development right into the home, enabling families to assess where their time and resources go, and to take charge of their own lives. Essentially, it shifts the focus of development work from 'things' such as assets, resources, and infrastructure to 'people' – from their daily activities, workloads, and interactions to their hopes and ambition. The approach has a starting point that households are not created equal; benefits and resources are shared differently. Women and men in the same family may pursue largely different livelihoods and have different responsibilities, which reap greater or lesser rewards. Often, the process reveals the roots of gender inequality.

Using these groundbreaking techniques, trained facilitators work either through groups or at the individual household level to help families develop a household vision of where they would like to be in three to five years' time. This inspires household members to assess their own situation and draw up step-by-step plans for a better future.

Through this process, family members often discover that gender inequality in the household is one reason they remain trapped in poverty. This can lead to negotiations and other members taking on some of the women's household chores so that the women can pursue activities that generate income for the benefit of all family members. Women and men are also encouraged to make changes outside the household by joining self-help groups and accessing financial services.

The first phase of using this approach in Malawi, Nigeria, Rwanda, Sierra Leone, and Uganda has reached some 100,000 people. Participants report improved productivity, higher incomes, less domestic violence, more resilience in the face of natural and economic shocks, more family harmony, and overall happiness. What's more, women gain more confidence, and their participation in decisions both inside and outside the home increases.

In my development career, I have seen many examples of the incredible achievements of rural women and their contributions to their families and communities. But let me close with one of the most recent – and astounding – examples. On a visit to China in June 2016, I met Zhang Danying, who had a small sewing business back in 2004 when the Qinling Mountain Area Poverty Alleviation Project came to her area. With a loan from the project she bought 30 sewing machines and hired 80 people (IFAD Stories, 2016a). She has never looked back. Though the project closed years ago, today Zhang's clothing company employs more than 200 people and earns more than 10 million Yuan (US$1.5 million) annually. She also started a poultry processing company that works along the whole value chain, from farming to the final packaging. The business employs over 1,100 workers (80 per cent of whom are women) and she has partnerships with 10,000 households who raise poultry for the company. In addition, she now runs a social welfare education centre for young entrepreneurs, most of whom are women.

That is transformation. And proof that investing in people can send ripples through a community that continue to touch lives and help more rural people even years after the formal development project has ended. That is the kind of sustainability we want so that we can reach the SDGs.

6.

Climate change: the time is now

During an address at IFAD's Governing Council, Pedro Tzerembo of the Shuar people of Ecuador said, 'Mother Earth is shedding blood. The sacred plants are dying. We have to protect the land of our children'. It was a moving address, one that commanded attention.

One of the many ways in which indigenous perspectives are powerful is the way they bring an issue into focus. And one of those issues is climate change. It is not just a matter of statistics or targets; it is something we have to feel personally, whether we are attuned to the environment around us or tuning in to the latest news reports. In particular, we need to think about the effects of climate change on agriculture, a subject that has not always been visible in climate debates. But the need is urgent.

The climate is changing before our eyes. Around the world, we are witnessing more extreme weather – from frequent floods, droughts, and fires to reduced average rainfall, increasing desertification, and declining soil fertility. Between 2008 and 2012, 144 million people were displaced from their homes by natural disasters, a number predicted to rise as global warming brings more extreme weather (IDMC, 2013). By 2016, more extreme and natural disasters were displacing on average 22.5 million people a year – equivalent to

62,000 people every day (IDMC, 2015). This movement of people can lead to local and regional instability. And when people are pushed away from rural areas and farming, it can threaten the food security of entire countries. This is why a goal of ending hunger (Sustainable Development Goal (SDG) 2) or of taking action on climate change (SDG 13) also means thinking specifically about rural areas. When we see pictures of flooded farmland, it is not only people's lives that are threatened – agricultural livelihoods and food security are being washed away.

Natural resources are coming under increasing pressure and competition. Water, one of life's basic necessities, is becoming increasingly scarce. Globally, 663 million people lack access to improved drinking water, and 8 out of 10 of them live in rural areas (WHO/UNICEF Joint Monitoring Programme, 2015). In 2015, it was estimated that 2.4 billion people globally had no access to improved sanitation facilities (ibid.). Global warming threatens to exacerbate these problems and the resulting tensions.

More than three-quarters of the world's poorest people live in the rural areas of developing countries. These are people with the fewest assets and the least resources to protect themselves against adversity. And they are the most vulnerable to unpredictable, erratic, and extreme climate conditions.

In other words, every day, those who have done the least to contribute to environmental destruction and climate change are the ones paying the biggest price. Everyone working in developing country agriculture has witnessed the impact of climate change on smallholder farming, including increasing crop and livestock losses. Yet the devastation – and its consequences for the planet – have not been fully appreciated.

Thankfully, this is starting to change.

A major step, of course, occurred in September 2015, when world leaders agreed on the SDGs, which will drive the global development agenda until 2030. At the centre of the SDGs are goals to eliminate extreme poverty, hunger, and malnutrition, and to preserve our planet. The need to raise the productivity and incomes of smallholders is highlighted.

Two months later, at the United Nations Framework Convention on Climate Change (UNFCCC) Conference of the Parties (COP21), world leaders reached consensus around the Paris Agreement – a bold plan whose aims include 'increasing the ability to adapt to the adverse impacts of climate change and foster climate resilience and low greenhouse gas emissions development, in a manner that does not threaten food production', and ensuring that climate finance supports those goals (UNFCCC, 2015).

As we pursue these complementary agendas, we must recognize the inextricable links between agriculture and climate change. In recent years, tangible progress has been made to mobilize finance for climate change. Little, however, has been directed at agriculture. This poses a grave risk for achieving the 2030 Agenda.

Smallholders are part of the solution

Too often, within the global conversation about climate change, agriculture is seen as a problem rather than a solution. In fact, it is both: while the agriculture sector is responsible for a quarter of global emissions, it also has the technical potential to offset a much bigger amount. Achieving this, however, will require economic and institutional incentives, as well as political will to promote green and low carbon development.

Within the agriculture sector, smallholders can play an incredibly important role, both in mitigation and adaptation. On the one hand, evidence shows that if we increase the carbon content in agricultural soils by even as little as 0.4 per cent per year, we can halt the annual global increase in CO_2 (von Kaenel, 2015). On the other, investments in adaptive and resilient smallholder agriculture are not only reducing vulnerability and increasing production, but also avoiding greenhouse gas emissions into the atmosphere. This is a triple win – not just for smallholders, but for everybody, including the urban populations that depend on rural people for their food.

No two smallholders are alike. But despite their diversity, they do share a vulnerability to climate shocks that affects their livelihoods and lives at various levels. Smallholder productivity depends on well-functioning ecosystems and their services. Many depend on rain-fed agriculture, for example. When changing weather patterns lead to longer dry seasons or extended rains, smallholders must adjust their farming activities. This, in turn, could add pressure to ecosystems through extracting too much water or using too many agrochemicals.

Some farms may simply not be able to adjust. Large farms and plantations with ample capital and resources, for example, may be able to weather the unpredictability of our changing climate. But smallholders, most of whom are poor, often lack resilience. Through no fault of their own, they may lack the assets and live too far away from services that could help them cope with extreme and unexpected weather. In addition, policy-related constraints such as unfair price regulation or poor extension services may hamper their ability to recover from shocks.

In India, smallholders make up over 80 per cent of India's farms (IFAD, 2011d). But more than half depend on rain, which arrives during the monsoons. In 2011, when the monsoon rains were delayed, the most vulnerable small farmers – those with fewer assets and less access to irrigation and weather information – were less able to respond than farmers who had greater capacity to adapt.

Land degradation also adds to the vulnerability of smallholders. According to the FAO, the world loses some 12 million hectares of land annually to drought and desertification (FAO, n.d. a).

FAO also predicts that climate change will negatively affect the fertility of arable land around the world. In sub-Saharan Africa, for example, up to 20 per cent of arable land may be less suitable for agriculture by 2080.

The same prediction holds true for drylands, which cover around 40 per cent of the world's land surface (UN Environment Management Group, 2011). These areas, which are extremely vulnerable to climate change, are inhabited by 2 billion people globally, and support the livelihoods of more than 200 million smallholders in sub-Saharan Africa alone (Walker et al., 2016).

Climate-smart agriculture

If smallholders are at risk from climate change, so too is global food security. To meet demand from a growing and more affluent population, we will need global food production to rise 70 per cent in less than 40 years (FAO, 2016b). Production in developing countries will need to almost double. Reducing post-harvest and post-marketing food losses may help meet some demand for food. The bottom line, however, is additional pressure to increase supply – at the precise moment that the varied impacts of climate change are jeopardizing what we can already produce.

During the first Green Revolution, the approach was relatively simple to increase yields: apply better seeds, increase fertilizer, and improve irrigation. The second Green Revolution will require more nuance to meet the challenge of feeding more than 9 billion by 2050. No magic bullet, no secret formula will allow smallholder farmers to respond to climate change and eliminate poverty and hunger overnight.

Climate-smart agriculture, or CSA, offers a triple win of improving smallholder productivity of nutritious crops, helping smallholders mitigate the impacts of climate change and adapting more effectively (FAO, n.d. b). CSA involves a range of approaches to build resilience and maximize the use of natural processes and ecosystems. In general, we must reduce excessive use of commercial fertilizers – though smallholder farmers are often so poor that they are hardly able to use fertilizers at all. And we must also diversify production, using a mix of traditional and new technologies.

I'm pleased that international policymakers increasingly recognize the merits of CSA. In 2014, following the United Nations Climate Conference in New York, the Global Alliance for Climate Smart Agriculture (GACSA) was launched to scale up climate-smart agriculture. With members from government, civil society, farmers' associations, and research organizations, among others, GACSA provides tools to assess how best to adopt CSA strategies – from practice briefs on intercropping, soil fertility, and manure to webinars on topics such as gender and agroforestry, mitigation in the livestock sector, and case studies on specific countries and regions (UN, 2014).

CSA encompasses many different approaches, each tailor-made to local communities, climatic conditions, and ecosystems. Typically, they maintain and enhance ground cover, enrich soil so it can retain nutrients and moisture, and enhance biodiversity. CSA leads to better yields, improved livelihoods, greater climate resilience, and reduced emissions.

These techniques are particularly well-suited to smallholder agriculture because they increase production and reduce poverty at the same time. I think of them as 'low-input, high-output, pro-poor technologies'. And they have worked throughout the developing world.

In many cases, CSA is about doing more with less. The International Rice Research Institute (IRRI), for example, is leading research into 'C4' rice, which will improve photosynthesis and thus allow sunlight into grain more efficiently. It has already increased yields by almost 50 per cent and increased the efficiency of nitrogen use by 30 per cent, all the while using less than half the water (IRRI, n.d. b).

But climate-smart agriculture goes beyond inputs, such as better seeds; it also depends on knowledge and innovative techniques – for example cropping systems that help farmers make the most of stress-tolerant varieties. In the dry areas of Nepal, an IFAD-financed project introduced short-duration leguminous crops along with upland rice (Adhikari and Rambaran, 2012). This approach both reduces the risk of crop failure and improves soil fertility at the same time. With evergreen agriculture, trees and shrubs are integrated with food cropping systems. This is a cost-effective and environmentally friendly method for increasing crop productivity and tolerance to changing weather patterns.

The use of shrubs has also helped increase yields of maize and cowpea in Kenya, and improved nutrient recycling and nitrogen fixation. The woody part of the shrubs can be used for firewood, stakes for crops, as animal fodder, or as mulch. This multiple-benefit approach also saves women time that can be invested in other farm or social activities. Finally, it reduces deforestation, a source of greenhouse gases (IFAD, 2015b).

To be successful, CSA requires changing attitudes about unsustainable practices such as cutting down trees for fuel and building supplies, over-exploiting other native plants, and tilling the land excessively through shovelling, hoeing, and raking. For generations, for example, many farmers have believed they need to plough the land to control weeds and pests, and to prepare seed beds. They will not abandon these practices simply because a researcher tells them that less tillage saves energy, time, and labour, or that it promotes healthier soils, conserves water, and reduces erosion.

In fact, there is growing evidence that climate-smart agriculture can generate impressive pay-offs. Research suggests that both adaptation and mitigation can have positive economic, environmental, and social spill-over effects for smallholders and their communities (Cooper et al., 2015). This message needs to reach smallholders all over the world.

When smallholder farmers in the Indo Gangetic Plains of India adopted zero-tillage systems, they counterbalanced their emissions by the carbon stored in the soil. Within three years, they became almost carbon-neutral. At the same time, these farmers increased their incomes by almost US$100 per hectare per year, mainly due to reduced costs of inputs and production (Aryal et al., 2015).

In parts of Africa where water is increasingly scarce, such zero-tillage projects have made smallholder farming viable again, while raising carbon levels in soils. Again, both smallholders and the planet share in the benefits.

Building climate resilience, then, involves not only research and 'hard' science, but also social science. In other words, farmers need to be engaged in the process, and given a reason to change. We can't expect them to alter long-held beliefs overnight – whether it's about reducing tillage or cutting down trees for food and fuel.

In the Sahel, IFAD has been working with small farmers and other rural people for more than a decade to value and nurture native trees and plants. This is particularly important during drought where evidence shows that re-greening activities lead to higher incomes and lower rates of infant mortality (Reij, 2009).

In Niger, for example, through the Farmer Managed Natural Regeneration (FMNR) technique, smallholders are re-growing trees and shrubs on agricultural land. It's a low-cost and simple technique with multiple effects – from protecting crops from heat, providing families with firewood, and allowing farmers to keep livestock, to enhancing biodiversity and combating desertification.

FMNR has resulted in some 200 million new trees on about 5 million hectares since the 1980s, representing about half of total farm land (ibid.).

IFAD has been proud to play a small role in Niger's success, supporting FMNR on more than 100,000 hectares in the Aguié Department. The programme, based on techniques developed by farmers themselves, has resulted in the growth of about 50 new trees per hectare in the area, which is now better protected from sandstorms (IFAD, West and Central Africa Division, Programme Management Department, 2014).

Today, Niger is far greener than it was 30 years ago. Researchers believe that several years of good rainfall have helped achieve these results, but that the main reason is the adaptation of farmers to the changing environment (Reij, 2009).

All over the world, I have seen with my own eyes how interventions with relatively modest investments, and with the participation of rural people themselves, are increasing resilience, protecting natural resources, and improving livelihoods. In a drought-prone region in Burkina Faso, I met smallholders using simple water-harvesting techniques, such as planting pits and permeable rock dams. They also integrated crops and livestock, creating a virtuous cycle for waste products: farmers can use animal manure to enhance crop production, and also feed crop residues to help boost animal nutrition and productivity. As a result, they restored land that was once degraded, and increased productivity (IFAD, 2011c).

Far away, in the South Gansu Province of China in 2013, I visited an area that suffers from frequent drought, limited water for irrigation, and severe soil erosion. Through basic, but effective, environmental practices such as harvesting rainwater, mulching maize, terracing, and planting trees to improve soil quality and moisture content, the farmers I met were not only feeding themselves and their families, they were also increasing their incomes (Paqui, 2011).

India's Maharashtra State also suffers from drought. Some 3 million farmers in the state depend on cotton for their livelihoods, but yields are low due to rocky conditions and soil erosion. The ongoing lack of rain increases problems with pests, which farmers typically address with commercial pesticides. An IFAD-supported project is showing farmers how to make natural pesticide out of local plants and to use animal dung to make fertilizer. These techniques won't make the rain come, but they do help preserve the existing harvest. Most crucially, they reduce costs. A year into the programme, participating farmers increased profits by an average of 42 per cent.

In the Peruvian Altiplano, the indigenous peoples have always contended with a harsh environment and extreme temperatures. In recent years, with climate change, temperature fluctuations and water shortages have become worse. Through an IFAD-supported project, local families are trapping water in pits for irrigation. They are diversifying their crops. They are planting trees for windbreaks and stabilizing the soil on the slopes. Perhaps most ingeniously, they are also using stones as heat reservoirs, soaking up warmth from the sun during the day and releasing it slowly at night to reduce freezing. In this way, they are producing more food than ever, and livestock is thriving (Rural Poverty Portal, n.d. a).

Yes, a stone can be an effective tool for resilience, not to mention a low-cost intervention. This example also shows that innovation sometimes takes unlikely forms and isn't just about high technology. Knowledge can be just as powerful; it also builds on the strengths that communities already have, because rural people living in challenging environments are well-versed in making the most of what they have, and doing a lot with a little. I explore these ideas more fully in Chapter 8.

Rural impacts of climate change

A key challenge of climate change is that the nature of extreme weather can vary from region to region. Some rice farmers in the tropics suffer from drought, for example, while others must contend with too much water. Every year, farmers in Bangladesh and India lose up to 4 million tons of rice due to floods – enough to feed 30 million people (IRRI, n.d. a).

IFAD has funded research and pilot projects that produce context-specific solutions to help farmers in numerous countries address the impacts of climate change. Of particular note, research carried out by the CGIAR centres with funding from the European Union channelled through IFAD has exceeded €233 m. In one of these initiatives – known as scuba rice – scientists at IRRI isolated the gene that controls tolerance to submergence, and developed a way for the gene to 'switch on' during floods (ibid.). Typically, when a rice paddy is flooded, the plant tries to escape the water by elongating its leaves and stems. High-yielding modern varieties cannot elongate enough, and literally wear themselves out in the attempt after a few days. Instead of struggling against the water, scuba rice preserves its strength for about 14 days, until the flood waters recede. Whether they touch on questions of flooding, drought, or salinity, such research projects have together reached hundreds of thousands of small farmers.

Projects to help smallholders address climate change come in many shapes and sizes, including efforts that mitigate climate change, while providing economic, social, and health benefits. The following example of methane shows how a single intervention can be a health, energy, and environment solution all in one.

Methane is a major contributor to climate change, generating emissions with a global warming potential 22 times more damaging than carbon dioxide (Rural Poverty Portal, n.d. b). It is produced in many ways, including through animal manure. When families cook on an open fire fuelled by animal dung, they release methane, and they also put their health at risk. Some 2.5 million people die every year directly from inhaling smoke from burning wood (IFAD Governing Council, 2013).

Around 2002, IFAD joined forces with the Government of China to pioneer the use of biogas, a clean, renewable energy obtained from biodegradable organic material such as kitchen, animal, and human waste. In remote communities of west Guangxi in Sichuan, where wood for fuel was in short supply and rural electricity was not available, an IFAD-supported project provided 'biodigester' tanks for biogas production, which convert animal manure into gas for cooking and for heating water (Rural Poverty Portal, n.d. b).

Each household involved in the project built its own 'plant' to channel waste from the domestic toilet and nearby shelters for animals – usually pigs – into a sealed tank. The poorest households, which had only one pig, built small units that could produce enough gas to provide lighting in the evening. Households with two or more pigs built larger units that could produce gas for cooking, as well as for lighting.

By 2006, the project had provided more than 22,600 biogas tanks, helping almost 30,000 households in more than 3,100 villages. Every year in the project area, 56,600 tons of firewood are saved, which is equivalent to the recovery of 7,470 hectares of forest (ibid.).

Poor people who were not on the power grid have reliable, renewable power for lighting, cooking, or even running generators. What's more, women, who once had to spend valuable hours collecting firewood, now have more time for their families and other activities. Children, who once could only read until night fell, can now pursue their studies in the evening at home. And all this investment in human health and quality of life is also less damaging to the environment. Indeed, when I visited Sichuan in China in 2009, I saw how the biogas project serves both to fertilize and irrigate crops. The sluice from the digester produced one of the healthiest and most luscious green vegetables I have ever seen.

The Guangxi project has become a catalyst for other initiatives in the region. To date, 2.73 million biogas tanks have been built in villages, benefiting about 34.2 per cent of the rural households in Guangxi. It is estimated that 7.65 million tons of standard coal and 13.40 million tons of firewood are saved annually in Guangxi because of the use of biogas (ibid.).

But the story doesn't end there. Through South–South cooperation, IFAD has taken the biogas technology into other parts of the developing world. In Asia and Africa, successful projects in Bangladesh, Cambodia, India, Kenya, Mali, Nepal, Rwanda, and Vietnam have introduced portable, ready-to-install digesters bringing electricity and cooking gas to homes in remote villages (IFAD, 2015d).

Clearly, through technologies such as scuba rice, biogas digesters, and many others, we can make a difference in the fight of smallholder farmers against climate change. We can help them build resilience. Perhaps most importantly, we can help build hope.

I have seen at first hand the impact of climate change on agriculture, and heard the voices of smallholders trying to cope. They speak of more frequent crop failures and livestock deaths, of food that is less available and more expensive, and of their fears for the future.

But I have also witnessed their inner strength, ingenuity, and readiness to seize upon opportunity. With access to often small amounts of support, smallholders can build their resilience to climate change and enhance food security.

Smallholder farmers suffer from climate change, but they are also part of the solution to it. However, climate finance has rarely reached them. IFAD's Adaptation for Smallholder Agriculture Programme, or ASAP, which was launched in 2012, is doing something about that.

Through ASAP, we make climate finance available to agriculture projects, aiming to increase the resilience of at least 8 million smallholder farmers, and ASAP is now the world's largest adaptation programme focused on smallholders. This is thanks to the generous support from nine bilateral donors that together have contributed US$350 m (IFAD Newsroom, 2014).

These funds make it possible to scale up proven approaches and technologies – from mixed-crop livestock systems and agroforestry to farmer information systems and sustainable watershed management. In so doing, we can increase agricultural productivity, while diversifying risk across different products. It allows us to build new investments in our programming that were missing in the past, such as early warning systems for pests and disease.

IFAD believes we can bridge the gap between agriculture, food security and climate change. We know it is possible to improve smallholder resilience, protect jobs, and reduce food insecurity, even in the face of climate change.

IFAD is one agency that has taken on the challenge of helping smallholder farmers respond to climate change. But obviously the world needs a more coordinated response, not to mention a massive scaling-up in line with the goals of the 2030 Agenda. This raises the question of how very large-scale goals – mitigation, resilience, adaptation – are to be carried out and interventions made effective at the level of the small farm. Without greater resilience for the small farm, global food security is under threat.

For decades, IFAD has specialized in targeted interventions to empower and engage with people who are often very poor and who live in remote and difficult environments. It can be done, and in fact must be done, since no 'universal' agenda can succeed if it does not reach the very areas where three-quarters of the world's hungry and poorest people reside. Partners need to adapt their business models, assess their delivery mechanisms, and build capacity of their staff to respond. All of us working in development must ask ourselves: 'are we fit to make a difference, especially in environmentally fragile and vulnerable areas?' It may not always be the case that we are; but it is certain that we can be.

As a scientist, I have seen how agricultural research can save money and lives. We need more investment in climate-smart research to help poor rural people produce more, and produce better – whether they are smallholders, pastoralists, fishers, herders or forest-dwellers. And then we need to make the investments necessary to get the benefits of those discoveries and new tools and techniques into the hands of rural people.

7.

Development starts at home

In the summer of 1981, I left my post with the International Crops Research Institute for the Semi-Arid Tropics (ICRISAT) in Burkina Faso to set up a regional station in Niger. We had 500 hectares of farmland, bushes, and shrubs to start research on dryland agriculture in the Sahel. Otherwise, there was nothing – no infrastructure, no buildings. We had to build everything from the ground up.

We drilled a well for water, set up some tents, and built five huts for our offices, quarters, and equipment. As team leader, I began making contacts with national and international organizations, as well as local farmers. It was really the beginning of my career. Starting from scratch, we created the biggest regional station outside of ICRISAT headquarters in India. We were putting Africa on the research map.

If only it had stayed there.

Think back to food security in the 1960s and 1970s. No one believed that India would ever be able to feed itself again. People in China were dying of famine. And Africa – Africa! – was providing assistance to the Republic of Korea.

At that time, many African countries were net exporters of major food crops. In my own home country of Nigeria, warehouses were bursting with cocoa and bales of silky cotton. Rivers were thick with floating timber primed for export. And the magnificent groundnut pyramids of Kano pointed towards a prosperous future.

Some African governments invested as much as 10 per cent of their budgets in agriculture (Adejumobi and Olukoshi, 2008). The continent had universities with agricultural faculties, research centres, and stations worthy of the name. Graduates from programmes in Egypt, Ghana, Kenya, Morocco, Nigeria, Senegal, and Uganda were some of the best in the world. Students even came from abroad to study there.

But while much of the world has moved forward, Africa slipped backward. Why? Many reasons, but I count among them the collapse of funding to agriculture, universities, and research centres, as well as the misplaced priorities of Africa's leaders. Those who fought to lead African countries from the bondage of colonialism to independence and statehood were replaced by greedy politicians who knew no better than to line their pockets.

Too many gains were reversed. Universities lost good people. The quality of education declined. To make matters worse, average global spending on agricultural research also fell.

Today, Kano is more likely known as the site of a terrorist attack than a symbol of national pride.

Is it any wonder there is so much poverty and hunger in sub-Saharan Africa? Yet Africa can be food-secure once again. I'm convinced of it. Investments of donors, the private sector and institutions like IFAD will remain critical. But the impetus for ending hunger and poverty must come first from within, and it must begin with agriculture.

For proof, I point to the case of Brazil, which relied on food aid and massive food imports in the 1970s. Today, the Ministry of Agrarian Development is strongly committed to combating rural poverty and creating a favourable environment for smallholder agriculture. Buying agricultural products from family farmers, for example, is a policy priority (IFAD, 2013f).

Policy is not enough, however. Despite the government's ambitions for rural areas, the poorest and most isolated populations had trouble benefiting from new financing and programmes aimed at smallholders. Among their many challenges, these smallholders needed to be better organized and develop higher quality products.

The IFAD-supported Dom Hélder Camara project responded to these challenges in the north-east region, one of the most disadvantaged in the country. The project strengthened the agricultural and small business management skills of farmers, helping them to improve quality standards. It also facilitated a strategic partnership between the community and Brazil's Zero Hunger Programme, which now buys produce from family farms to supply schools and hospitals (Rural Poverty Portal n.d. j). Not only did the project build capacity in a disadvantaged region, it also fed back lessons learned into the design of further public policies (IFAD, 2013f).

Why can't African countries follow a similar path? Many African economies are growing strongly, but too often this is on the back of extractive industries that do not yield jobs and income for Africa's poor and hungry. You cannot drink crude oil. You cannot eat diamonds or gold.

The path to modernity and inclusive prosperity must pass through fields and pastures. That is both metaphor and truth. Across the centuries, it is agriculture that has given the first impetus to economic growth – from England in the 1700s, Japan in the 1800s, and India in the 1900s to Brazil, the Republic of Korea, and Vietnam in the new millennium.

But building an enabling environment for agriculture to prosper is more difficult now than in the past. The world's population is over 7 billion and will be well over 9 billion by 2050, with much of that growth in Africa. Countries already struggling to harness their potential in agriculture are also faced with the impacts of climate change – from prolonged droughts and higher temperatures to extensive flooding.

To complicate matters further, many countries have become more fragile through conflict. In Eritrea, Mali, Niger, the Democratic Republic of Congo, Somalia, and others, conflict has choked agricultural and livestock production, along with markets and trade flows. As a result, millions of women and men have been deprived of their livelihoods. Fewer people to work the land and raise livestock only further limits access to and availability of food.

But these obstacles can, and must, be overcome. Yes, there are giant external forces that impact the trade fortunes of developing countries. There is thus a continued need for advocacy work to remove subsidies and barriers put in place by industrialized countries. The bottom line, however, is that development starts at home.

National-level governments alone cannot solve a country's problems. But neither can they step aside and expect the private sector, other levels of government, and civil society to do all the heavy lifting. Working in partnership, governments can listen to the needs of their people, and act accordingly – such as by creating favourable policy environments so that rural businesses can thrive.

Enabling rural transformation

What kinds of policies create an enabling environment for agriculture to flourish? The answers will provide only part of the equation for success, and there will be variations from place to place, because policies are only as good as a government's commitment to them. For that reason, I would argue that one cornerstone for development must be good governance.

Trade agreements and regulations may exist, but are of little value if they are not enforced. Enforcement requires strong political will to eliminate illegal practices. But eliminating corruption and reducing risk, unpredictability, and uncertainty of return on investment are essential to bringing other players on board who can help propel countries and communities toward development.

For example, foreign investors look for environments where governments are prepared to defend the foundations of democracy and safeguard the political stability so critical to economic growth. They look for governments with the strong political will to eliminate illegal practices, whether these occur at border crossings or in the offices of elected officials and bureaucrats.

Investors don't like surprises. They need consistent and predictable policies that will not change in response to short-term shocks. Governments, then, need to go beyond short-term thinking.

I would like to see traditional five-year plans give way to truly long-term visions that extend 25 or even 50 years. Of course, such plans would need to be adjusted along the way. However, at their essence, they would form a pact between developing country governments and investors, and be a commitment to creating and maintaining an investment climate for agriculture.

Land: a right and prerequisite for smallholders

Many critics of foreign investment point to 'land grabs' whereby corporations obtain huge tracts of prime land from developing countries. Even if these investments target the agricultural sector, their large farms and plantations may devastate the landscape, while retaining most of the profits.

In this scenario, the fault does not lie necessarily with foreign investors. If someone comes into my home to rent a room, and instead I give them my bedroom and go to sleep on the veranda, then I can only blame myself. By the same token, if foreign countries and companies are buying up large tracts of land, developing country governments have to look at themselves in the mirror. Once lost, this land may be hard to regain.

A nation's land is a strategic reserve for a country, part of its legacy. Protecting it may result, in the short term, in lost opportunities. But in the long term, the policy will ensure that government maintains control over the use of land and works only with those companies prepared to respect the terms of agreement. Rising food prices since 2008 have shown both the public and private sectors that agriculture can be a source of prosperity and growth. That growth, however, needs to be inclusive.

Governments must take care not to mortgage their countries' future through ill-advised sales to foreigners. It is one thing to permit or encourage legal financial flows, however, and another to turn a blind eye – or willingly abet – illegal financial flows. The Africa Progress Panel has found that corruption and lack of transparency in Africa are pervasive, undercutting progress on many levels. Illicit outflows from Africa totalled some US$75 bn in 2013 alone (Kar and Spanjers, 2015).

Corruption hurts everyone. It makes ordinary Africans pay higher fees for education, health, and business services. It increases business costs, undermining efficiency and job creation. And it destroys the fabric of still-fragile democracies, feeding cynicism about leaders who use public office for private gain.

But good governance, like development itself, cannot be imposed from the outside. Integrity, too, begins at home.

If poor rural people had stronger rights to their land, would it be so easily 'grabbed' from them?

Land is fundamental to the lives of poor rural people as a source of food, shelter, income, and social identity. When people have secure access to land, they are less vulnerable to hunger and poverty. But competition for land is fiercer than ever, driven by a host of factors, ranging from a rising global population to the impacts of climate change.

There is no easy solution to secure land rights. Should rights be formal or informal? Statutory or customary? Permanent or temporary? Private or common? Legally recognized or traditional?

The options are obviously complex and fraught with consequences. Poor rural people, for example, often have more control and influence over land use through common-property systems than through legally registered individual land rights.

As a result, it can sometimes make more sense to strengthen traditional administrative systems than to create new, formal systems of land ownership. Here, we can fall back upon the proven power of people-centred development. When in doubt, ask the 'stakeholders' themselves! Ultimately, we need to empower poor rural people to take part in developing land policies that positively affect their lives and livelihoods.

This idea of engaging and empowering poor rural people lies at the heart of IFAD's work around land tenure (IFAD, 2012d). We collaborate with governments, civil society organizations, development institutions, and other partners on ways to strengthen poor rural people's access and tenure.

Our tools include recognizing and documenting group rights to rangelands and grazing lands, forests, and artisanal fishing waters; recognizing and documenting smallholder farmers' land and water rights in irrigation schemes; strengthening women's secure access to land; using geographic information systems (GIS) to map land and natural resource rights, use, and management; and identifying best practices in securing these rights through business partnerships between smallholder farmers and investors.

In Madagascar, for example, poor rural people have traditionally been barred from owning land (ibid.). In the mid-2000s, the national government introduced a simple certification process to improve land tenure security. As part of its support for this process, IFAD-funded projects have helped poor rural people secure the necessary identity papers to apply for a land certificate (ibid.).

In Nepal, where community forestry has been widely promoted, efforts to secure tenure for poor rural people are also helping to regenerate degraded forests. In collaboration with FAO, an IFAD-supported project enabled groups of the poorest people in highland villages to obtain long-term leases to severely degraded forest areas. Building on achievements in the first phase, more than 4,000 leasehold forest user groups were formed, involving more than 38,000 households. The groups received leases for almost 20,000 hectares of land (ibid.).

The results are impressive. A 2009 study found that 69 per cent of the plots had been rehabilitated, and that household income over the project period had increased by more than 70 per cent. In addition, indigenous peoples and low-caste groups had benefited proportionately more than higher-caste households, which was the project's intention (ibid.).

IFAD has understood that equitable access to land and tenure security are key to eradicating rural poverty. This is a message that we deliver to policymakers through various channels, including our work with the Global Donor Land Working Group, the Global Land Tools Network, and the International Land Coalition (ILC). In 2015, for example, ILC members implemented 79 national land policies and agendas, organized 13 campaigns, and mobilized more than 35,000 people to advocate for land policy changes in their countries.

As a result of the ILC's work, more than 84,000 farmers now have more secure land tenure (IFAD, 2015a). The ILC also promoted inclusion of land rights in the 2030 Agenda and indicators for measuring them. While the Millennium Development Goals (MDGs) made no mention of land rights, the Sustainable Development Goals (SDGs) have four targets that refer to land tenure and rights.

Working with its partners, IFAD contributed to the formulation of the Voluntary Guidelines on the Responsible Governance of Tenure of Land, Fisheries and Forests in the Context of National Food Security (VGGTs). These guidelines were officially endorsed by the Committee on World Food Security in 2012 (FAO News, 2012). IFAD also helped develop the Principles for Responsible Agricultural Investment, which cover such issues as recognition of existing land rights, strengthening food security, transparency and consultation, and respect for the rule of law (Committee on World Food Security, 2014).

The question of land tenure can be complex, sensitive, and highly politicized. But through multi-stakeholder dialogue – which gives voice to poor rural people – we can support better land governance. I would also argue that private-sector investors can play a stronger role in this process through mechanisms such as the International Land Forest Tenure Facility (IFAD, 2015e).

The role of the private sector

When it comes to agriculture, the private sector is, by turns, elevated as a saviour and castigated as a bogeyman. If development truly does start at home, the private sector is certainly an important member of the 'family'. And under the right conditions, it can help this family thrive.

Most of all, we need to recognize that small farmers are already part of the private sector. As I argued in Chapter 3, farming at whatever scale is a business. To make a sustainable business, you don't need pity or handouts; you need investment. This is as true of smallholder farming as of anything else.

The idea of public-private partnerships is no longer novel. Yet traditional '3P' relationships tend to overlook the critical role of producers, and often fail to mitigate risks and transaction costs. As a result, IFAD now adds producers into the equation. Such 4P partnerships benefit farmers by providing links to secure markets, as well as access to technology, services, innovation, and knowledge. And the private sector gains by having access to reliable supply and spreading risk across a large number of small farms.

We must ensure that smallholders, especially women, are not excluded, exploited, or otherwise marginalized from business opportunities. For companies, this may mean working with farmers' organizations. These groups can act as a single point of contact, simplifying operations and paperwork for companies, while offering a degree of protection for individual farmers.

Cocoa farmers in São Tomé and Príncipe, for example, are now supplying chocolate makers, including companies in Europe (Rural Poverty Portal, n.d. f). In the Pacific, small farmers are supplying organic virgin coconut oil to The Body Shop in the United Kingdom. This success is allowing more children to attend school and funding a way of life that incorporates health, ecology, fairness, and care (Rural Poverty Portal, n.d. h). These partnerships bring together the interests of all parties in ways that are mutually beneficial, equitable, and transparent. But for the private sector to take its rightful seat at the table, government needs to set out the chairs and make the rules.

Government also plays an essential role in providing the public spending to improve rural infrastructure, education, energy services, and agricultural research and development, as well as improvements in governance needed to drive transformation.

These are areas where government has not only a 'comparative advantage', but a responsibility.

Working in partnership, government can support the development of inclusive financial systems that serve everyone. Financial services rarely reach into remote areas, leaving many rural people without efficient payment systems, safe savings and credit institutions, and facing high transaction costs for financial services. Through partnership, we can build relationships between organized small-scale producers and private companies, negotiating and supporting inclusive and sustainable collaboration.

IFAD plays an important role as an investor and as a broker between the private sector, government, and smallholders themselves. It collaborates with research institutions to promote innovation, and then brings this knowledge into its investment projects. But for all of this to happen, government's role remains critical, as factors such as regulation, infrastructure, and education lie largely within its domain.

In Moldova, where 60 per cent of the population live in rural areas and depend on agriculture for their livelihoods, IFAD has been helping to develop carefully tailored rural financial services (Rural Poverty Portal, n.d. i). This supports the government's priority of reducing poverty through agriculture and rural development, and helps address a tremendous need for credit in rural areas.

IFAD financing makes it possible to provide loans to small- and medium-sized rural businesses through commercial banks and non-banking microfinance institutions. While the banks themselves issue the bulk of rural credit under short-term maturities, IFAD makes credit available for up to eight years. This gives farmers and entrepreneurs the possibility to draw up business development plans over the longer term and build their enterprises with solid financial support.

IFAD-supported projects have kick-started any number of enterprises – from those that produce noodles for traditional chicken broth to those that make dairy products like sour cream, *kefir* and yoghurt (Rural Poverty Portal, n.d. d). In 2012, a loan recipient in Moldova beat more than 250 other organic producers from 26 countries to win top prize at an international forum for a variety of gouda herbal cheese known as 'queen'. At the forum, the company, Heuverland SRL, also signed contracts with importers from the Russian Federation, Turkey, and Ukraine (Rural Poverty Portal, n.d. g). Who could have predicted such success?

In the end, it is investments made by millions of rural micro, small and medium enterprises that will primarily drive the transformation we want to see in rural areas across the world. By using domestic and international public funds in innovative ways to leverage these investments, we can achieve a large-scale and lasting impact on poverty and hunger reduction. In the process, we can create a world where more families live in dignity, and young people realize their aspirations for a better life in their own rural communities.

No single entity – whether public or private, including smallholders themselves – can succeed on its own. But working together we can create partnerships that are sustainable, productive, profitable, and inclusive. Rural areas need not just *more* investment, but the *right kind* of investment. Attention should be given to developing the domestic private sector for rural people to thrive. It does not make sense to give tax waivers to multinationals when our own commercial banks deny our domestic private sector access to finance. How can they compete with foreign investors when special privileges are meted out to one group of investors? Do African small and medium enterprises ever receive similar treatment? Yet they are the largest private sector group on the continent!

Fortunately, we are starting to see progress with governments tailoring national policies to the needs of local communities.

In Burundi, for example, the government introduced fertilizer subsidies and increased the share of the budget to agriculture from 3.6 to 10 per cent between 2010 and 2012 (IFAD, 2013b). In Panama, an IFAD-supported project provided economic and logistical support for negotiating laws for indigenous people's land rights (ibid.). In Sierra Leone, IFAD helped build a rural banking network from the ground up after the end of the civil war (Beavogui, 2010). And there are also encouraging developments with Ethiopia's Agricultural Transformational Agency (UNSGSA, 2013) and Tanzania's Growth Corridor (IFAD, 2014d).

I applaud the trend towards corporations seeking a social contract with local communities. Such agreements – if they are honoured on both sides – will ensure that investments not only provide local jobs, but also build a community's resilience through support for social services like health and education, as well as greater environmental protection.

Beyond the horizon

For a variety of reasons, most smallholder farmers do business only in their local markets. This is only natural. But while development begins at home, it must also look beyond the horizon to expand. Many smallholders certainly have products that could be sold on markets further afield, but infrastructure or transportation problems make that prohibitively expensive or outright impossible.

According to the 2014 Africa Progress Report, sub-Saharan Africa was a net exporter of food before 2000 (African Progress Panel, 2014). By 2011, African countries were spending US$35 bn to import food (excluding fish) (ibid.). Meanwhile, the share accounted for by intra-African trade was less than 5 per cent (ibid.).

One reason African farmers can't engage beyond local markets is lack of infrastructure. But roads can be paved, storage facilities can be built, and electricity capacity can be installed. What's more, it can often happen with the support of the very private investors that the agricultural sector needs in order to flourish. Other blockages depend on government action, including tariffs, customs procedures, and rules of origin, which can lead to lengthy and costly wait times for transit and shipping, especially for smaller companies.

We must help African farmers tap into regional and continental markets. This is important for economic reasons, and can also mitigate the impact of price volatility and improve food security. Trade between African nations can ensure that food is available throughout the continent, even when climatic shocks disrupt production.

Intra-regional trade in Latin America and the Caribbean also remains low: just over 19 per cent of exports are exported within the region (ECLAC, 2014). But efforts are underway to transform the region. Not so long ago, Brazil was a net food importer. In just 30 years, however, it has become one of the biggest producers and exporters in the world. The creation of the Brazilian Agricultural Research Corporation (EMBRAPA) played no small role in this transformation. Working with other national and state-level institutions, EMBRAPA showed how institutions can bring policies to life, transforming agriculture and economics.

Governments must create a policy environment that allows small- and medium-sized enterprises and agro-industries to develop and flourish. With this enabling environment in place, smallholders need support to help them compete in domestic, regional, and international markets. For example, smallholders and processors may need training to help improve managerial skills and meet the sanitary and phyto-sanitary standards required by supermarkets for their increasingly demanding customers. Thus we see that governments make policy, and policy affects every aspect of smallholders' livelihoods. The link can be direct and obvious, as with policies around land and access to resources. But that is not all.

When I talk about the need for more investment in research, I stress that research for the sake of research is wasteful and pointless. But ultimately, research must have practical applications; to make the transition from the lab to the field, we need enabling policies that can connect research to products and markets, and that link researchers with the global storehouse of knowledge.

There are already splashes of hope in Africa. The Forum for Agricultural Research in Africa (FARA) has launched a Science Agenda for Agriculture in Africa (FARA, 2014). Owned and led by Africans, the Science Agenda holds out the promise of African farmers and citizens reaping the benefits of African research. If supported by coherent government policies, it could translate into stronger nations and better lives. In another encouraging development, the New Partnership for Africa's Economic Development (NEPAD) launched its Comprehensive Africa Agriculture Development Programme (CAADP) to strengthen food production and security (NEPAD, 2003).

I was there and witnessed the heyday of African research from the 1960s and 1970s. From personal experience, I know scientists need the right incentives, both financial and material, to work in their home countries. They also need modern equipment to do their jobs, and must be linked to global knowledge networks and institutes. Good science also needs to be cultivated.

When I look back at how little we had starting up the ICRISAT research centre in Niger, and how little I knew about administration, it's a wonder that we had the wherewithal to survive and grow. But for me, then as now, failure was not an option.

Today, the permanent buildings resemble an oasis in the desert – a testament to our commitment to home-grown African solutions to agriculture. Development can, and should, begin at home. This is why, in June 2014, I issued an open letter[1] to African leaders urging them to fulfil the promise of investing in rural agriculture:

> *Judging from the daily outpouring of commentary, opinions and reports, you would think that there were two African continents. One of them is the new land of opportunity, with seven of the world's 10 fastest-growing economies, offering limitless possibilities to investors (The Economist, 2011). There is, however, this other image: a starving and hopeless continent, hungry and poor, corrupt and prey to foreign exploiters.*
>
> *As Africans, we are tired of caricatures. But we are also tired of waiting – waiting to be led towards the one Africa we all want, the Africa that can and should be. We know the real Africa, filled with possibilities, dignity and opportunities, able to face its challenges and solve them from within. Never has the time been more right for us finally to realise our full potential. It is within our grasp.*
>
> *As a scientist, I am always interested in facts. Africa is a land rich in resources, which has enjoyed some of the highest economic growth rates on the planet. It is home to 200 million people between the ages of 15 and 24 (Agbor et al., 2012). And it has seen foreign direct investment treble over the past decade.*
>
> *As the head of an institution whose business is investing in rural people, I know that you also need vision and imagination. At the International Fund for Agricultural Development we have banked on the poorest, most marginalized people in the world, and over and over again these investments have paid off for people and for societies. And more than half the people we invest in are Africans.*

---

[1] The letter appeared in numerous news outlets, including *The Guardian*, *The Huffington Post*, *Jeune Afrique*, and the *Nigeria Sun*.

Almost 11 years have passed since the Maputo Declaration, in which you, as African leaders, committed yourselves to allocating at least 10 per cent of national budgets to agriculture and rural development – key sectors in the drive to cut poverty, build inclusive growth, and strengthen food security and nutrition (NEPAD, 2003).

Today, just seven countries have fulfilled the Maputo commitment consistently, while some others have made steps in the right direction (ONE, 2013). Eleven years is a long time to wait. I have seen projects turn desert into farmland in less time.

In just a few days, in Malabo at the 23rd African Union summit, I will join those of you, African leaders, who will gather to discuss this year's topics – agriculture and food security. This is my call: don't just promise development – deliver it; make it happen now. Make real, concrete progress towards investment that reaches all Africans, investments that prioritize rural people.

Our biggest resource is our people. To squander this is worse than wasteful. If we don't act now, by 2030 Africa will account for 80 per cent of the world's poor (Africa Progress Panel, 2014). Is this the legacy that we want to leave for future generations?

The AU declared 2014 to be the year of agriculture and food security. And this is the year we look beyond the deadline of the millennium development goals to a post-2015 world with new goals and targets to reach. I hope this means that we will be dedicating ourselves fully to making agriculture a priority. GDP growth due to agriculture has been estimated to be five times more effective in reducing poverty than growth in any other sector, and in sub-Saharan Africa, up to 11 times (FAO, IFAD, and WFP, 2012). Paradoxically, it is countries that lack lucrative extractive industries, and which have had to invest in agriculture, that have found out what is now an open secret: agriculture not only improves food security but also creates wealth. Small family farmers in some parts of our continent contribute as much as 80 per cent of food production (FAO, 2008). Investing in poor rural people is both good economics and good ethics.

A full 60 per cent of our people depend wholly or partly on agriculture for their livelihoods (FAO, 2012a), and the vast majority of them live below the poverty line (World Bank, n.d. c). It's not pity and handouts that they need. It's access to markets and finance, land tenure security, knowledge and technology, and policies that favour small farms and make it easier for them to do business. A thriving small farm sector helps rural areas to retain the young people who would otherwise be driven to migrate to overcrowded cities, where they face an uncertain future. Investing in agriculture reinforces not only food security, but also security in general.

In an Africa where 20 states are classified as fragile (World Bank, n.d. b) and 28 countries need food assistance (FAO, 2016a), the need for a real rural transformation backed by investment and not just words is critical – I have often said that declarations don't feed people.

Investment must be focused on small family farms. Such smallholdings make up 80 per cent of all farms in sub-Saharan Africa. And, contrary to conventional wisdom, small farms are often more productive than large ones. For example, China's 200 million small farms cover only 10 per cent of the world's agricultural land but produce 20 per cent of the world's food (HLPE, 2013). The average African farm, however, is performing at only about 40 per cent of its potential (Opportunity International, n.d.). Simple technologies – such as improved seeds, irrigation, and fertilizer – could treble productivity, triggering transformational growth in the agricultural sector. It is estimated that irrigation alone could increase output by up to 50 per cent in Africa (You et al., 2011). Rural areas also need the right kinds of investment in infrastructure – roads, energy, storage facilities, social and financial services – and enabling policies backed by appropriate governance structures that ensure inclusiveness.

If we look at the countries that have met the Maputo commitment, we see that investing in agriculture works. Given that agriculture has become lucrative for private investors, and that about 60 per cent of the planet's available uncultivated agricultural land is in Africa, there is no mystery about why we hear of so-called 'land grabs' (Leke et al., 2010). Opportunity draws foreign investors. There is nothing wrong with foreign investment. But it has to be managed, for the benefit of all.

What is a mystery is why, with such vast potential and a young population just waiting for a reason to seize it, our African leaders do not announce that they will redouble their efforts to drive an inclusive rural transformation, with concrete commitments, that will make Maputo a reality. I hope that, after the Malabo meeting, that will be a mystery no longer.

African economies have grown impressively. But it is time to stop focusing on GDP figures and instead focus on people. The majority of our people are engaged in agriculture, and the neglect of that sector must stop if we really want to realize the healthy, peaceful, and food-secure Africa that we know it can be. It is not a dream: it is a responsibility.

Kanayo F. Nwanze
20 June 2014

(Nwanze, 2014).

Two years later, I continue to urge leaders in Africa to fulfil their Maputo commitments and invest in the rural development that Africa so desperately needs. With the right policies and support, smallholder farmers can use new knowledge, technologies, and infrastructure to drive sustainable development. Rural transformation starts at home.

8.

Science, technology, and innovation

My father, who was a headmaster in various government-run schools in Nigeria, had a dream that I would one day become a medical doctor. The University of Ibadan accepted my application for a first degree in science, which would be the foundation for medical school. But with the chaos of the Biafran War, I had to postpone my studies for years. By the time I finally enrolled, the university would not guarantee my choice of faculty. And so, I began to study agriculture – an unexpected path, but one that I would not change.

Agricultural science is science with a purpose. We always have to ask ourselves how it will be useful in improving the lives of people and food security. In other words, we must reposition research *and* development so that it is research *for* development. This means measuring our results not by higher yields alone, but by reduced poverty, improved nutrition, cohesive societies, and healthy ecosystems.

To that end, we must be bold in pushing the frontiers of science, innovation, knowledge, and experimentation and not shy away from questioning the logic and sequence of events and processes. When the situation dictates, we must challenge scientific conventional wisdom and think outside the box.

This should not be so difficult. Scientists are full of big ideas and dreams of changing the world. They envision new varieties of crops that can resist disease and pests, perform well in extreme weather conditions, or heighten productivity. And through dogged persistence, and sometimes good fortune, they often realize those dreams.

Yet the most exciting innovations do not always emerge from a laboratory. They also come – quite literally – from the ground up through the experience and ingenuity of smallholder farmers who know their land better than anyone else. Good development, then, marries the 'hard' natural sciences and the 'softer' social sciences that reach out to farmers and take a people-centred approach to finding solutions.

Technology and innovation

While in India, I saw how the International Crops Research Institute for the Semi-Arid Tropics (ICRISAT)'s Genome Centre for Excellence was sequencing the pigeon pea genome – a legume that provides protein for more than a billion people in the developing world. The draft genome sequence has an alpha-numeric code, but it's commonly known as *Asha*, which in Hindi means 'hope' (Varshney et al., 2012).

Hope, indeed. This research has the potential to revolutionize the development of plants, making them higher yielding and faster maturing, but also disease-resistant and tolerant to drought and other stresses. It is exciting work – a big dream that may one day transform our world.

I have a special place in my heart for the work by ICRISAT. I joined the Institute in 1979 as principal cereal entomologist in Ouagadougou, Burkina Faso, the beginning of an 18-year career with them that spanned assignments in Niger and India. My experiences with the institute provided the foundation for my work at WARDA, now known as the Africa Rice Center.

As Director General of WARDA in the 1990s, I championed New Rice for Africa, or NERICA, a project to produce a rice variety that combined the high productivity of Asian rice with the hardiness of local African varieties. Rice is a staple of the African diet, but the wild varieties that grow well in sub-Saharan Africa are low yielding.

My former colleague, Dr Monty Jones, had tried for years to cross a hardy African rice – *Oryza glaberrima* – with a high-yielding Asian species – *Oryza sativa*. Crossing wild species is not a simple matter, and his success rate was very low. Then, Dr Jones went to China and was shown a method of using coconut oil in cultures. He tried it with his interspecific crosses, and his success rate rose to around 50 per cent. The rest is history.

Today there are dozens of NERICA varieties. They mature quickly, demand less labour, and they are drought-tolerant. NERICA is a boon to farmers and to everyone who depends on it for food. Farmers have seen yields rise by 25 to 250 per cent (FAO, 2002). In 2004, Dr Jones's work on NERICA was recognized when he was co-awarded the World Food Prize (World Food Prize, n.d. a).

NERICA was the product of biotechnology and molecular science through which we transferred genes from the Asian species of rice to the African one. This approach, which falls under the umbrella of agricultural biotechnologies, has its critics. Many associate it with genetically modified organisms (GMOs) and the subgroup of GMOs known as transgenics, about which I too have concerns. These categories, however, should not be confused.

With our changing climate, crops will need to be more resilient to extreme weather conditions, heat, floods, and droughts. In some cases, farmers will need to change the crops they grow, and people will need to change their diets. We can help farmers adapt to a changing climate by using the benefits of science to target the needs of poor and food-insecure populations (as was done with

NERICA) as well as by using a people-centred approach that takes into consideration the social context.

We can do this without the use of transgenics as well. For example, since 2007, the European Union (EU), in partnership with IFAD, has been funding scientific research that helps rural people adapt to the effects of climate change and improve food security. Developing new seed varieties is one area where new research can have a major impact, but to help rural people adapt to climate change, sometimes an entirely different cropping system is needed as well.

For example, in parts of Kenya and the United Republic of Tanzania, producers and consumers have traditionally preferred maize to other grains, despite its relatively low levels of nutrition (IFAD, 2015b). As water resources grow scarcer, however, these communities have been faced with consistently failing crops. The solution here is neither development of drought-tolerant nor early-maturing maize varieties, but a decision that farmers must make: for instance, a change in farming systems from maize to sorghum.

Sorghum requires half as much water as maize, affords greater nutritional benefits, is drought- and heat-tolerant, matures early, has the ability to withstand water-logging and grows in areas where other crops cannot. With the EU-IFAD funding, ICRISAT has developed high-yielding drought-, pest-, and disease-tolerant sorghum varieties and hybrids. ICRISAT has bred more than 15 improved sorghum varieties that have reached 100,000 farmers in Kenya and the United Republic of Tanzania. In the targeted arid and semi-arid lands, sorghum yields have doubled. By completion of the current support in 2018, these improved varieties will have reached a further 100,000 farmers (ibid.).

I am always in favour of a transparent and open debate. But we should ask ourselves whether the debate on GMOs for African smallholder farmers makes any sense. To what extent have farmers exploited existing, time-tested, 'old-fashioned' technologies (such as irrigation, high-yielding varieties, and fertilizers) that can triple, if not quadruple, yields? And what then do farmers do with the surplus produce – feed rodents and storage pests, when there are no roads to the next market town? When farmers lack the means to store and transport a surplus to market, this potential boon becomes food waste. As I describe later in this chapter, we cannot dissociate science and technology from traditional knowledge and local innovation. A people-centred focus and attention to context go a long way in guiding us to the right solutions.

Accessing global knowledge can also help provide solutions for local problems. During the late 1970s and 1980s, for example, in sub-Saharan Africa, crop losses for cassava – a staple food for more than half a billion people in Africa, Asia, and Latin America (CGIAR, n.d.) – were as high as 80 per cent. The culprit was *Phenacoccous manihoti*, better known as the cassava mealybug. This insect was accidently transported from its home in South America to Africa in the 1970s. Within 15 years, it had spread across most of the continent, putting at risk the lives of millions of people who depended on cassava for their survival (Donnelly, 2008).

At the time, as a young entomologist, I was on my first field posting in the Democratic Republic of Congo, then called Zaire. While researching ways of controlling the pest, I decided to do something considered innovative for the time: instead of exploring new synthetic pesticides, I researched insects that could prey on the mealybug without damaging the crop.

In 1978, I travelled to the then Commonwealth Institute for Biological Control (CIBC) in Trinidad and brought back several species of predatory wasps (*Anagyrus lopezi*) on a pilot basis. I left Zaire shortly after returning from Trinidad, but the approach was expanded by Hans Herren and others, and became the foundation of a successful Africa-wide control programme. By 1988, the mealybug threat was under control throughout Africa, saving at least 20 million lives (World Food Prize, n.d. b), and around US$2.2 bn in production (Norgaard, 1988). The cost of this programme was only US$20 m – in other words, one life was saved for every dollar invested, without any adverse effects on the soil or to human health. This work was recognized in 1995, when the World Food Prize was awarded to Hans Herren (ibid.). It also demonstrates how global knowledge can provide solutions that address local problems.

Technologies that can improve agriculture also go beyond agricultural technology, per se, to include various existing technologies that can be used in innovative ways. Smartphones and tablets were not made with smallholder farmers in mind, for example, but have nevertheless become indispensable tools to gather information and obtain knowledge. In Cambodia, IFAD joined forces with Intel to bring new digital tools to smallholders (IFADTV, 2014). They allow farmers to analyse soil and other conditions on farms so they can use appropriate seeds, fertilizers, and pesticides. The software will even help locate the nearest suppliers!

Sometimes the results are surprising. Often, we speak of farmers who lack inputs such as fertilizer, and how this affects crop yields. But in some cases the opposite is true. For one Cambodian farmer, the Intel tool revealed she had been overdosing her rice fields with fertilizer. Reducing these inputs allowed her to cut her costs in half (ibid.).

We should pause a moment to consider this example. Digital technology has revolutionized modern life, but some have been left behind. It is time for us to consider how they can catch up to enjoy the same benefits. Once we get beyond the outmoded image of smallholder agriculture as primitive, subsistence agriculture, we can think about how technological advances could change the lives of the people who work these 500 million small farms. Whether it takes the form of e-wallets and mobile banking, or tablets and other such devices, digital technology can connect smallholder farmers to worlds outside their villages. The Ethiopian Agriculture Transformation Agency, for example, is using new technologies to create a digital soil map of the country (Ethiopian Agricultural Transformation Agency, n.d.).

The gap between rural areas and urban centres is shrinking. They are ever more connected. In the future, as I discuss in Chapter 10, small towns will play a key role in further bridging the gap. What is called 'decentralized urbanization' is already encouraging inclusive growth in many areas. It includes decentralization of some kinds of manufacturing to rural areas and towns, as well as growing urban demand for the goods and services produced by the agriculture sector.

Even as we pave dirt roads to strengthen access to markets, we must also be aware that building capacity in a community entails more today than traditional infrastructure, schools, and health clinics: it also means building virtual communities where farmers can learn from their peers around the world. Sustainable agriculture has been called 'knowledge intensive', and we should be conscious of all that 'connectivity' implies. Apart from providing knowledge, access to the global knowledge and communication network can help farmers organize, find common cause, and voice their concerns to policymakers.

These connections further show how the Sustainable Development Goals (SDGs) are not really separate; they are different aspects of how we need to direct development to reach a sustainable future.

And rural development cuts across all of them. For example, SDG 7 refers to clean and affordable energy (UN General Assembly, 2015b). Rural people need to harness energy to take advantage of modern technology, build infrastructure and improve their lives. Yet the *Africa Progress Report* in 2015 highlighted that 600 million Africans do not have access to modern energy, due to a variety of factors including corrupt utilities, wasteful subsidies, and chronically bad policymaking. Worse, it was projected that sub-Saharan Africa was 'the only region in which the absolute number of people without access to modern energy is set to rise' (Africa Progress Panel, 2015: 16).

Obviously, this future is incompatible with reaching the SDGs. Energy will be as important as water and land in transforming rural areas; without such a transformation, we won't be able to make the productivity increases that will both help eliminate rural poverty and ensure future food security.

Thus, attention to rural needs reminds us that we not only need to look at the SDGs, we need to look *across* them. This can be a challenge when you think of a development landscape with a welter of agencies and mandates – which is why we need partnerships more than ever.

Technology that works for people

And that brings me back to the necessity of a people-centred approach. When you take your cue for development by looking at the challenges that people face in their lives, by talking with them and involving them in charting their own path to development, you avoid some of the problems with top-down approaches. It is not always an easy or smooth process. In some cases, scientists who have discovered or adapted effective and useful technologies still find it difficult to convince smallholders to adopt them. And the reverse is also true. In some cases, farmers themselves come up with the big ideas, and scientists are reluctant to accept them.

Take the system of rice intensification (SRI), which aims to increase yields in irrigated farming with approaches that challenge conventional practices. IFAD tested SRI in countries like Burundi, Rwanda, and Madagascar, where it was developed in the 1980s (IFAD, 2012e). I have personally met farmers in Rwanda and Burundi who have doubled rice production using SRI.

Yet despite this successful adoption all over the world, some rice scientists have rejected SRI. They were trapped in a mindset that rice production had to mean flooded rice. This approach is common in Asia, which has some of the world's largest producers and indeed produces and consumes almost 90 per cent of the world's rice (Papademetriou, 2000). Yet upland rice cultivation accounts for much of production in Africa, making SRI a viable approach (Oteng and Sant'Anna, 1999).

The 'hard' sciences know the value of observation in controlled conditions, but when we are dealing with innovations or advances that are meant to improve people's lives, we have to think about context. The softer social sciences complement laboratory and experimental work with real-world knowledge. Smallholders have much to teach us if we open our minds – they may lack formal education, but they know the terrain and the social context where a new technology might work. To boost the productivity of smallholders, our work must start with learning their beliefs, cultures, and other local variables. A new 'Green Revolution' will need to be significantly different from the last, with more focus on participatory approaches and sustainability.

For all the power of new technologies, a simple 'back to basics' approach often works best. In many developing countries, for example, optimizing conventional approaches, such as micro-dosing of fertilizers and micro-irrigation, can yield dramatic results. Often, a community suffering from poor irrigation for their farms does not need a team of engineers with the latest equipment, or large-scale and capital-intensive interventions. Much can be accomplished with a rock dam that stabilizes soil and collects water run-off, or with cisterns that collect rainwater. And it can be done with and by rural people themselves.

The ingenuity of people and the spirit of innovation came together in a pilot project in Madagascar. Many poor Malagasy in rural areas wear plastic flip-flop sandals, which are practical for walking through dust and water. However, flip-flops eventually break, and once cast aside, they end up in landfills or are simply discarded. This is not a story about waste management, but rather about micro-irrigation and empowering smallholder farmers.

Malagasy farmers are generally traditional. They do not easily adopt new farming technology – unless they can be convinced it will be successful (Center for Evaluation, 2012). An IFAD supported micro-irrigation initiative set up 97 demonstration projects in 60 rural communities to show the benefits of drip irrigation kits and liquid organic fertilization kits. While supporting vulnerable farmers, the project – known as SCAMPIS – also aimed to build the capacity of local business to produce kits that were better adapted to local needs and more affordable (Rural Poverty Portal, n.d. c).

The old flip-flops became part of the solution, because they could be ground up and turned into raw material to manufacture parts for micro-irrigation equipment. Remarkably, this inexpensive, locally produced equipment transformed the lives of vulnerable farmer households by allowing farmers to improve crop production. At the same time, the project created jobs, both for street workers who collected the old sandals, and for small businesses that made the irrigation parts. Beneficiaries were able to increase their revenues, partly because the micro-irrigation systems saved them time. In the most successful examples, poor women vegetable growers significantly increased their cash flow, and improved household food and nutrition security (ibid.).

Local solutions can often take root where projects that were drawn up thousands of miles away without community involvement may fail. And this is an important lesson for the implementation of the 2030 Agenda; its goals may be universal, but reaching them will require context-specific and locally-owned solutions. Repurposing flip-flops will not 'fit' the needs of every community in Madagascar or elsewhere. Even so, a number of IFAD-supported initiatives replicated the micro-irrigation approach, especially in the southern region, which experiences regular water shortages. By mid-2012, nearly 4,700 families in the initial project area benefited from the technology. With scaling up in other Malagasy zones, the number of beneficiaries rose to some 9,300. Furthermore, the approach was scaled up and implemented in other parts of the world (ibid.).

The numbers of households benefiting from a technology, or the small businesses that received support, are certainly valid and important measures of impact. But there are also less tangible impacts, which remind us that development is about changing human lives for the better. In interviews with evaluators, farmers involved with SCAMPIS noted that using micro-irrigation technology allowed them to return from the field less dusty and dirty. This made them feel better about themselves, strengthening their self-esteem and heightening their dignity (Center for Evaluation, 2012).

Lest anyone imagine that this is an insignificant co-benefit, consider that the global average age of a farmer is about 60 years (FAO, 2014). Attracting a new generation to farming is essential to meet future food security needs, and presenting farming as a dignified and profitable profession will be key to that.

A similar low-cost, elegant, and brilliantly simple solution is using old bottle caps to more effectively dispense fertilizer. With support from ICRISAT, farmers in sub-Saharan Africa are learning to use them to micro-dose fertilizer (ICRISAT, 2001). Micro-dosing is not so much about using less fertilizer as using it efficiently, which is both cost-effective for the small farmers and better for the environment. Such grassroots, local techniques are being taken seriously by the research community and need to be among our toolbox of interventions as we take the 2030 Agenda forward.

ICRISAT worked with farmers in the semi-arid regions of the world struggling with infertile soil and low yields. They knew that many farmers desperately need chemical fertilizers. But they also know these inputs are expensive and harmful to the environment if used excessively. A bottle cap was found to hold about 6 grams of fertilizer – an optimum amount needed per seed (ibid.).

Farmers in several countries, including Niger, Burkina Faso, and Zimbabwe, used the bottle cap method to apply small, affordable quantities of fertilizer in the hole where the seed is sown. The fertilizers and the moist environment encourage root growth and improve the germination rate of the seed. Stronger root systems capture more water in the soil, increase crop yields, and reduce the plants' susceptibility to drought.

This may seem a very homely solution compared with the sophisticated use of technology to accomplish the same goal of titrating fertilizer use that I described in Cambodia. But it works, and once again shows that a ground-up, people-centred approach can identify successful solutions where top-down development may fail.

Sceptics may wonder if simple techniques using the materials at hand can be scalable – that is, can we possibly achieve a universal agenda calling for the eradication of hunger and poverty by such means? This is a valid and important question. The experiences discussed here show that we can.

In fact, when you work with people to involve them in their own development, you find that they already possess a wealth of knowledge and indigenous solutions. Farmers in the past often invented simple technologies that, for one reason or another, subsequent generations abandoned. Innovation, then, can mean reviving or adapting a traditional practice rather than creating something completely new.

The Farmer Managed Natural Re-Generation (FMNR) approach illustrates this point well. This IFAD-supported project worked with local farmers in Niger to revive and improve the traditional practice of using planting pits and 'half-moons' to rehabilitate degraded land. Farmers dig the pits to collect and store rainfall and run-off. The half-moons are earth embankments in the shape of a semi-circle; these are much larger than the pits, and can also capture run-off water (IFAD, 2011c).

The results in the village of Batodi in Niger are impressive. Twenty years ago, the fields around Batodi were almost barren. Today, using these traditional technologies, the fields have higher on-farm tree densities. The soil is more fertile and the trees provide fodder for livestock. Furthermore, the increases in well water levels suggest that water harvesting techniques have recharged the groundwater. In 2011, the village had 10 gardens around the well (Reij, 2012). Several had become permanent, allowing crops to be grown throughout the year. This allows villagers with access to gardens to better cope with drought than those without access.

Although the project ended in 1996, farmers here still used these techniques in 2012. Thankfully, none of their children had died during the famine in the previous year. The ability of poor people to grow and feed themselves during one of the worst droughts in living memory using simple water harvesting techniques shows the power of simple ideas. They can, in fact, save lives.

Another example, which I saw for myself, was in Zhang Cheng Pu village in South Gansu province, China. The area suffers from frequent drought and limited resources. I saw how villagers had used many small pieces of mirror to make a solar dish, and used the solar energy to boil water! This technology is easily transferred to any part of the world with abundant sunlight.

In the Pacific nation of Tonga, which encompasses 45 separate islands, another kind of local solution was found. The 30 inhabitants in the remote Lape community live three hours from the main island of Vav'ua (Rural Poverty Portal, n.d. k). In Lape, where access to the harbour was difficult, people carried sweet potatoes, *pandanas* (a material used by the women to make woven goods), animals, and even injured villagers on their backs. For them, the solution was a Chinese invention dating back millennia: the wheelbarrow. The reasoning was that not only could wheelbarrows go where there are no roads; they would also not need fuel and were easy to fix.

A group on Lape raised the money needed to apply for a grant from an IFAD-supported programme known as Mainstreaming of Rural Development Innovations, or MORDI (ibid.). With four wheelbarrows, they could transport goods more easily to the harbour. They also use the tool to transport the sick and injured to the harbour more quickly and more comfortably when necessary to leave the island for a hospital. What's more, wheelbarrows have bought villagers freedom and time, reduced women's drudgery, improved earnings, and created employment.

For farmers in developing countries, who inhabit remote and under-resourced communities and are often living on difficult terrain, the local home-grown or traditional solution is right when it's the solution that works. The high-tech solution is right if *it* works. Each puzzle has its own dynamics, demanding tailor-made approaches that reflect the resources at hand, and the context.

IFAD's decades-long experience working with rural people at ground level shows that innovation starts with an open mind, and finding what works – whether it's as modest as old flip-flops and bottle caps, or recycled shards of a mirror, or as advanced as biotechnology, GIS maps, and mobile phones to access weather reports, virtual banking, and market news. Once you know what works, you can build partnerships to scale up those solutions. Thus, development can deliver for – and with – the people who have been bypassed before, but now must be at the very heart of the universal agenda.

9.

The cost of inaction

In his Nobel Prize laureate lecture in 1970, Norman Borlaug – the plant biologist known as the father of the Green Revolution and the man who saved a billion lives – spoke eloquently of the 'privileged world' and the 'forgotten world' (Borlaug, 1970). The forgotten, although they number 2 billion, are mostly invisible.

More than three-quarters of the world's poorest children, women, and men live in the rural areas of developing countries. They are deprived, underprivileged, and hard to reach because they often live in remote areas. The rural poor, who overwhelmingly depend on agriculture for their livelihoods, lack access to markets, finance, technology, services, and infrastructure that would allow them to thrive. What's more, their struggles remain largely unseen.

In Africa, nearly a third of the rural population lives more than five hours away from a market town of 5,000 people (Livingston et al., 2011). It has been estimated that upgrading the main highway network in sub-Saharan Africa could expand overland trade by about US$250 bn over 15 years, with major benefits for the rural poor, including for smallholder farmers. But lack of road infrastructure acts as a disincentive to invest in increasing production, because it makes it difficult if not impossible to transport a marketable surplus to the consumer (World Bank, 2009).

The world does not see their daily struggles because persistent indignity and lack of opportunity do not make headlines. Yet, as I argued in Chapter 2, inaction on poverty and hunger is a prime driver of migration. When a crisis becomes simply too large to ignore, the forgotten get the attention of the world's political and media centres; but once the crisis passes, they slip back off the agenda.

In all my years of working in development, I have never seen food security stay as high on the global agenda as it has since the 2008 food crisis. I would like to think the world has accepted that meeting this basic human need is fundamental not just to achieving the Sustainable Development Goals (SDGs), but to our survival. One could even hope that the consensus on the 2030 Agenda signals a recognition that our short term and our long term have merged; problems like climate change, hunger, conflict, and poverty must be solved now.

While I am far from cynical, I am realistic. Now that the goals have been staked out, investment must follow.

We can work to keep food security on the global agenda in two ways.

First, we must show food security is connected to achieving all the Sustainable Development Goals (SDGs). While SDG 2 focuses directly on the question, and calls for the world to 'end hunger, achieve food security and improved nutrition and promote sustainable agriculture', food security is intimately tied to many of the other SDGs. Among these are SDG 3 (Good health and well-being), SDG 4 (Quality education), SDG 11 (Sustainable Cities and Communities), and SDG 15 (Life on Land), to name only a few (UN General Assembly, 2015).

If a child does not have enough nutritious food, how can she grow into a strong and healthy adult? If her belly is empty, how can she concentrate enough to obtain a quality education?

If we neglect our rural areas so much that youth migrate to urban centres, how can we grow food in the future? And if migrants overwhelm the limited absorption capacity of urban areas, what will become of the agenda of building sustainable cities and communities? If we do not support rural transformation, how will we manage our forests sustainably, reverse land degradation, or halt the loss of biodiversity?

The second aspect is to stop thinking of rural areas as remote and disconnected to urban life. Rural areas have always supplied food and other goods to cities, but the rural and urban spheres are increasingly interconnected. In this ever-shrinking world, where desperation, disease, and violent ideology know no boundaries, we must insist that the problems of the forgotten and invisible are our problems as well.

Learning from Ebola

The Ebola crisis of 2014-15 offers a poignant illustration of this, as well as of the terrible cost of inaction. Ebola, an infectious and often deadly virus, was first discovered in 1976 after outbreaks in Sudan and the former Zaire. The scope of the 2014 outbreaks in West Africa, however, dwarfs those early cases both in size and complexity. In the space of 16 months, the virus killed over 11,000 people, almost all in Guinea, Liberia, and Sierra Leone (WHO, 2016).

As well as being a health crisis, Ebola crippled the agriculture-based economies of those three West African countries and undermined food security. Farmers stayed home, leaving their fields to rot. In Sierra Leone, for example, up to 40 per cent of farms were abandoned in the worst-affected areas (UN Economic and Social Council, 2014).

The Food and Agriculture Organization of the United Nations (FAO) estimated that the crisis affected more than 1 million people (FAO Emergencies, 2016). Development agencies were forced to intervene to assist the three most-affected countries to rebuild their agricultural systems (Das, 2016). The price of food rose, while productivity and household income fell, creating shortfalls in tax and non-tax revenue for the three countries. These losses were considerable for countries experiencing fragility and recovering from conflict.

The direct and indirect costs of the Ebola crisis and its aftermath are mind-boggling. According to Save the Children, the international effort to contain the outbreak in Guinea, Liberia, and Sierra Leone cost an estimated US$4.3 bn (Save the Children, 2015). By April 2015, according to the World Bank, the Ebola crisis continued to cripple the economies of the three countries, even as transmission rates showed significant signs of slowing. It estimated the countries would lose at least US$2.2 bn in foregone economic growth in 2015 as a result of the epidemic. This figure, high as it is, does not include extra costs for emergency relief, nor the millions of dollars in costs to nations not directly afflicted by Ebola.

Even from this brief summary, it's clear that these three countries stumbled at the starting gate of the 2030 Agenda. All those targets – from ensuring healthy lives and achieving food security to ending poverty and ensuring economic growth – were put further out of reach as the countries struggled desperately not to slip backwards.

What caused the crisis to spread unchecked? A major factor was poor rural infrastructure – good hospitals, trained personnel, and sound information were lacking. In addition, many trained medical and other personnel were among the first infected, creating an extra burden.

Yes, it would have cost a great deal of money to build up health systems to handle such an emergency more effectively – estimates run at US$1.58 bn. But this is a small fraction of the US$4.3 bn that was invested to deal with the crisis after the outbreak (ibid.).

Apart from practical considerations, such as health infrastructure, the fact that the crisis was brewing in regions that were typically ignored by the privileged world, and was affecting people who were largely invisible, also helped the virus spread unchecked. To be blunt, the threat to rural lives and the unspeakable human cost in lives lost and families torn apart did not matter enough to the rest of the world for it to respond rapidly and strategically to the devastation wrought on isolated agricultural communities.

What sparked action was the appearance of Ebola in the capital cities of the three countries, followed by its arrival in Europe and the United States. Then the privileged world began to quake, fearing a broader epidemic, which led to a collective global response. The veil lifted, and the forgotten were suddenly visible. But too often, once a crisis is past, the veil falls once again, until the next time.

Yet we cannot lay the entire blame for the epidemic at the feet of the privileged world for not having reacted sooner. In Chapter 7, I argued that development begins at home. Preparing the ground for people to succeed – and to survive, if disaster strikes – requires foresight and investment, both public and private, in every country, whatever its challenges or level of development.

Where are the leaders?

In many countries of Africa, the easy profits of oil and mining promised national wealth without the hard work of building and maintaining the social structures on which stability, commerce, and the rule of law depend. Rural areas and agriculture suffered in particular. As millions of dollars found their way into private bank accounts, opportunities for millions of rural people disappeared at the same time. Then, when energy prices fell, revenue declined and the same countries found themselves even less equipped to respond and maintain their food security.

Nor is this practice limited to Africa. According to the *Extractive Industries Transparency Initiative (EITI) 2016 Progress Report*, only about 15 per cent of revenue from the mining and hydrocarbon sector in Peru has been used for developmental spending, such as infrastructure or economic diversification. The rest has been used on current expenditures, such as salaries and servicing debts. With the country's involvement in EITI, however, local citizens have more information to engage with regional authorities on alternative ways to spend these resources (Extractive Industries Transparency Initiative, 2016). In this way, once overlooked communities can gain greater visibility and, perhaps, influence policy.

When a government allows the hopes and dreams of its most marginalized to vanish, is it any wonder these poor rural people remain invisible and forgotten? If countries do not see their own rural people, how can we expect the rest of the world to open its eyes?

The State of Food Insecurity in the World 2015 found that many countries have failed to reach the international hunger targets (FAO, IFAD, and WFP 2015). Natural and human-induced disasters or political instability have resulted in protracted crises. This has only increased vulnerability and food insecurity for large parts of the population.

We need to break the cycle of individual tragedies becoming collective disasters. This will require political leadership, robust policies, investments in infrastructure, social safety nets, healthcare, and, of course, strengthening of the agricultural economy. This is especially true of sub-Saharan Africa.

In 2003, at the African Union Summit in Maputo, African leaders pledged to reverse their longstanding underinvestment in agriculture. A decade later, fewer than 20 per cent had followed through on their commitments to allocate at least 10 per cent of national budgets to agriculture and achieve 6 per cent annual agricultural growth (ONE, 2013).

There is another choice: to transform African agriculture and build inclusive, fair societies, with opportunities for their children and grandchildren. Thankfully, some countries are taking this path. Between 2005 and 2009, for example, Ethiopia averaged growth of 9.5 per cent in the agriculture sector and exceeded the Maputo target for expenditure on agriculture. For its part, Ghana has averaged 5.5 per cent agricultural growth in recent years. At the same time, it has steadily approached middle-income status, following unprecedented reductions in poverty. It is one of just three African countries to have already reduced hunger by half (ibid.).

Africa's leadership must take the blinkers off, or go down in history as the generation that allowed Africa's economic success to benefit just a select few, while hundreds of millions of Africans remained desperately hungry, poor, and forgotten.

The Intergovernmental Committee of Experts on Sustainable Development Financing estimated that around US$50 bn would be required annually to eliminate hunger by 2025 (United Nations Intergovernmental Committee of Experts on Sustainable Development Financing, 2014). The United Nations System Task Team Working Group on Financing for Sustainable Development projected that an additional annual investment of at least US$50 bn would be needed for sustainable development related to land and agriculture (UNTT Working Group on Sustainable Development Financing, 2013).

Those are staggering figures, but our alarm should be tempered by the knowledge that billions are spent on the global defence trade each year, and that illegal financial flows and trade cost billions more. These huge sums are a testament to the damage inflicted by poor governance, misplaced priorities, and simple greed.

It is, of course, important to ask where we will get the resources we need for development. But we should also think about how we are investing the resources we already have. Do fiscal choices bring the worlds of the privileged and the forgotten closer together, or push them further apart?

Malnutrition, an avoidable tragedy

It is troubling to think that a crisis like Ebola must reach the privileged before the world takes notice. Often, other crises are bubbling under the surface whose impact may be even more devastating, both socially and economically. What will it take for us to see them?

Consider the blight of malnutrition, which is caused by inadequate, excessive, or imbalanced intake of carbohydrates, protein or fats (macronutrients) and vitamins and minerals (micronutrients) (IFAD, 2014c). Undernutrition is the largest contributor to child mortality worldwide. Nearly 25 per cent of children under five are stunted (UNICEF, 2013). In South Asia and sub-Saharan Africa, home to three-quarters of these children, the figure is 40 per cent (ibid.). Almost 800 million people were undernourished in 2015 (FAO, IFAD, and WFP, 2015).

Every day more than 8,000 children die from preventable causes related to undernutrition (Horton and Lo, 2013). Those who survive early malnutrition may suffer lasting consequences. Children chronically malnourished in the critical first 1,000 days, beginning at conception, can suffer irreversible damage to their physical and mental development (UNICEF, 2013). In 2011, there were 165 million children with stunted growth, leading to compromised cognitive development and physical ability (ibid.).

Micronutrient deficiencies (lack or excess of specific vitamins and minerals) affect a staggering 1 billion people in addition to those suffering from undernutrition. No wonder the lack of micronutrients such as iron, vitamin A, zinc, and calcium is called 'hidden hunger'.

Surely the cost of inaction on malnutrition is too high, both socially and economically. Over their lifetimes, malnourished individuals can earn 10 per cent less than well-nourished ones. Every year, it's estimated that Africa and Asia lose an amount equivalent to 11 per cent of their gross domestic product to undernutrition (IFPRI, 2016).

Think of all those goods and services that could, and should, have been produced. All those billions of dollars in productivity lost due to malnutrition. In addition, governments end up spending billions of dollars on programmes in order to deal with poor nutrition and its effects.

Good nutrition is thus not just an outcome of economic growth and social development, but an essential input as well. Investing in nutrition through agriculture is more than a social good. It is sound development policy and good economics.

The challenges of achieving good nutrition, however, are increasingly complex. With urbanization, consumption patterns are changing. Even in the low- and middle-income countries where IFAD works, people are consuming more processed foods and leading more sedentary lives. As a result, diseases related to obesity and diet, such as heart disease and diabetes, are becoming more common. At the same time, in many of these same countries, adult undernutrition and micronutrient deficiencies persist.

There is broad agreement that SDG 1 – ending poverty everywhere – cannot be achieved without dealing with nutrition. Improving the nutrition of farming populations not only reduces the number of undernourished people, but also increases agricultural productivity and contributes to a thriving agricultural economy. Thus, nutrition is central to combating rural hunger and poverty and achieving rural transformation. The simplest of campaigns on nutrition should start with rural households: 'You are what you eat' and 'What you grow is what you eat'.

This may seem obvious, but in fact agriculture – not to mention the role of smallholder farmers – has been missing from debates about nutrition. IFAD's work brings the benefits of agriculture to bear on the problem of malnutrition. The projects we support help shape agriculture and food systems in ways that improve the nutrition, incomes, and productivity of smallholders and the rural poor. Agricultural development enables smallholders to grow more food – and in particular more nutritious food – for themselves and their families. Developing their livelihoods can also increase their incomes, which can enable them to buy a greater diversity of nutritious foods than they themselves produce. And by affecting food systems as a whole, these efforts benefit the entire population – rural and urban alike.

Improving nutrition also means understanding and supporting the role of women. Women make up a large percentage of the workforce in agriculture and food systems in developing countries. Along with productive and reproductive gender roles, women's education, social status, health and nutritional status, and control over resources are key factors that influence outcomes on nutrition.

Gender-sensitive agricultural projects can ensure that women retain greater control over resources and have a say in the choice of crops. Preparing and cooking meals, carrying water, working in the fields or at the family business, as well as multiple other activities create significant demands on a woman's time and energy. When agricultural investments empower women and promote gender equality, they allow women time to take care of their children and other family members. At the same time, they provide time for women to engage in other economic and entrepreneurial activities, which are in turn empowering.

IFAD is mainstreaming gender into all its projects, recognizing the key role that women play in agriculture, rural communities – and nutrition. In eastern Indonesia, for example, the IFAD-supported Coastal Community Development Project works with 70,000 fishing households in areas of high poverty. Many women had little or no opportunity to earn money, yet their husbands' incomes were barely enough to support their households. Through the project, women have been able to access loans and technical support to start their own businesses. One group of women, for example, started a small processing business, which produces fish floss (a dried fish product), fish nuggets, and fish crackers. Overall, among project participants, incomes have increased by an average of almost 60 per cent. Some of the profits are invested in the business, and the rest are shared among group members (IFAD, 2015a).

Experience has shown, however, that higher incomes do not necessarily translate into better nutrition outcomes. Attention to education and information, for example, are essential to ensuring that expanded and more diverse production leads to the adoption of healthier diets and promotes better nutrition, particularly for smallholders. Similarly, without social and behavioural changes, food storage and preparation and diets may stay the same, even if incomes, production, and productivity increase.

The Addis Ababa Action Agenda (AAAA) recognized the contribution rural development can make across the SDGs. At the same time, rural development itself involves action across many sectors, including health, water and sanitation, and education. For that reason, IFAD takes a multi-sectoral approach wherever possible.

In Laos, undernutrition leaves every second child with stunted growth, making them small for their age, leaving them more vulnerable to illness, and creating learning disabilities. IFAD worked with the national government, as well as with UNICEF and the World Food Programme, to develop the country's first coordinated multi-sectoral response to undernutrition, engaging the ministries of agriculture, health and education.

Our work in Laos combines agriculture, nutrition, and education in an innovative way. In addition to providing seeds for beans – a good source of protein – IFAD helped create a television soap opera called *My Happy Family* to spread the word about nutrition. Storylines in the programme, for example, touch on the use of local plants and vegetables as sources of micronutrients. They show parents the need to create separate meals for children and adults. Since a young child can't digest sticky rice, she is better off eating sweet potato porridge, wild vegetables, and fish (IFADTV, 2016b).

What do soap operas have to do with development? In this case, quite a lot. The Laos project looked at everything from what people grew to what they ate and how they lived, and how they received information. Its point of departure was the actual lives of rural people.

In Bangladesh, IFAD provided a grant to the World Fish Center (one of the CGIAR centres) to explore if farming nutrient-rich small fish could increase household incomes and improve nutrition. Initially, fishers were concerned that raising both large and small fish in the same ponds would hurt production. In fact, the studies found that technologies to raise small and large fish together actually increase total fish production (IFAD, 2014c).

Finding concrete evidence and changing behaviour, of course, are two separate challenges. If fisherfolk can be convinced the approach works, they could raise the nutrient-rich small fish – *mola* – in the 4 million small, seasonal ponds in Bangladesh. By consuming *mola*, more than 6 million children could meet the annual recommended intake of vitamin A (ibid.).

Investing in action

The above examples illustrate how ending hunger (SDG 2) is not simply a matter of growing more food, or even growing more nutritious food. Understanding social and cultural barriers and opportunities plays a huge role in achieving success. The challenge is, in part, to make the right investments that reach rural people, even in isolated communities, with the tools and the knowledge not just to increase production, but also to eat better.

What constitutes the 'right' investments? There is no single answer because each situation is unique. Still, nations have much to learn from each other if we give them the chance. In many cases, diverse countries and communities can find common ground in their social, political, economic, and environmental challenges – enough to share approaches and adapt solutions.

In our work in 98 countries across Africa, Asia, and Latin America, IFAD has seen first hand, the value of South–South cooperation, as well as the role middle income countries (MICs) are playing in international development, as donors and trading partners. This value comes not only through sharing the tried-and-true, but also through innovation through mechanisms such as Embrapa — the Brazilian Agricultural Research Organization (IFAD, 2011e).

Over the last six years, for example, IFAD has provided financing to support Embrapa's 'Innovation Marketplaces' in Africa and Latin America. This mechanism uses an online platform to provide grant funding on a competitive basis. It makes it possible for development practitioners and researchers in Africa and

Latin America to solve specific problems by drawing on Brazil's agricultural expertise (Benchwick, 2010).

By 2016, the Marketplace had raised some US$20 m from its partners and financed around 80 projects in 13 African countries and eight countries in Latin America. Around 1,000 germplasms have been exchanged, 1,200 experts have been trained, and 150 technologies and services shared (Agricultural Innovation MKTPlace, n.d.).

Investment, whether in sharing existing solutions or creating innovative new approaches, offers no intrinsic guarantee of advancing the cause of smallholder farmers. For that reason, IFAD invests in rural transformation, encouraging both social and economic change that provides poor rural farmers with a range of opportunities for decent and dignified lives. All of us stand to gain when there is a flow of goods, services, and money between rural and urban areas and when nations can have balanced growth that embraces both the visible and the invisible.

In the nearly 50 years since Norman Borlaug described the breach between the privileged and the forgotten, the problems of the invisible world have become too glaring to ignore. We have seen the international community ultimately respond to Ebola and other crises. We have got through them, though thousands died. But a response, by definition, is passive. Instead, we need to anticipate, and act coherently before the next crisis arrives.

The contribution of agriculture and food security to achieving the 2030 Agenda is indisputable. We need rural areas to grow our food, and to maintain the healthy ecosystems that contribute to the clean water and air we all need. Cities have a finite capacity. They cannot provide good jobs, housing, and sanitation for every person. We do not need bigger cities with bigger slums. Rather, we need a world where populations, employment, services, and opportunities are more evenly distributed.

That may not sound like an emergency, and yet it is. The realities behind the 17 SDGs may look more or less urgent, or threatening, but in total they represent a generational challenge that must be met. And nowhere is that more visible than in the gaping divide between the visibly better off urban areas of the world and the neglected rural spaces, which we depend on yet often ignore.

The cost of action is high, but inaction is higher still. It can be measured by the direct and indirect cost to economies, by the devastation inflicted on the natural environment, and by the suffering and needless death of the most vulnerable people. In our increasingly globalized world, the lives of the privileged and the forgotten are more connected than ever before. We forget this at our peril.

10.

The future of farming

The world is becoming increasingly urban, yet towns and cities are still fed by people working the land in rural areas. Given the lack of resources and lack of access to markets faced by many rural people – particularly women, who make up nearly half of the developing world's farmers – there is little incentive for them to increase productivity.

The mass migration and urbanization happening today are symptoms of conflict, insecurity, injustice, inequality, and lack of opportunity. Every day, short-term interests and short-term thinking leave millions of children, women, and men – especially in rural areas – with few options. Often, they will leave everything behind for an uncertain future elsewhere.

Who can blame them? If farming is seen only as a back-breaking and unrewarding activity, if there are few resources to increase production and no markets, even if more was produced, it is hardly surprising that young people and others leave their homes in search of a better life.

Migration is a rational response to a world that is unequal, unsafe, and unsustainable. People need other reasonable choices, but this will take an integrated approach to poverty, hunger, and food insecurity – one that addresses issues of rights, equality, inclusion, and good governance, alongside an economic and an environmental agenda.

When people are given choices, many choose to remain in rural areas. In north-east Brazil, for example, where a million rural families struggle to grow anything on dry, toxic soil, an IFAD-supported initiative is transforming the lives of people like Ulisses dos Santos and his family. Water from their shower, sink, and toilet had been flowing untreated from their house. Now grey water passes through a biofilter made of pebbles, grit, wood shavings, and humus with earthworms, cleaning the water enough to use as irrigation. This has led to better sanitation, higher agricultural yields, better nutrition through a diversified diet, and even a surplus to sell to increase their income. Like many young farmers, Ulisses had been contemplating a move to the city in search of work. The biofilter system, however, is allowing him to make a living in his community (IFADTV, 2012). In other words, there is one less migrant drifting into an overcrowded metropolis, one more family given the tools to pursue their dreams at home.

The rural–urban nexus

What does the ideal agricultural system of the future look like? I would argue that the 500 million family farms in the developing world will remain the backbone of global food security. But the small farm of the future needs to evolve with the times. It needs an enabling environment, access to technology and markets, off-farm opportunities, and a new generation of young people getting into farming. A world in which the Sustainable Development Goals (SDGs) are met will have to have vibrant small farms and rural communities as a central feature. Perhaps, above all, achieving the SDGs will depend on a more holistic understanding of the relationship between rural and urban areas.

Human beings tend to divide things into simple contrasting pairs: night and day, good and bad, rich and poor. In the field of development, time and again we see the apparently neat spatial division between rural and urban. But the reality is far more complex.

A more accurate picture of people's lives in rural and urban areas would show that rural and urban areas are increasingly interdependent. Poverty today is predominantly rural, with more than three-quarters of extremely poor people found in rural areas. However, the absolute number of urban slum dwellers is growing, with an estimated 828 million people currently living in slum conditions, compared to 767 million in the year 2000 (UN, 2010). And although rural people produce food, many of them are also net buyers of food, just like their urban counterparts (IFAD, 2011a). And rural off-farm business and employment are increasingly important.

In today's rapidly urbanizing world, the rural–urban split is more accurately represented as a continuum than a divide. We need to move beyond binary thinking, finding ways to forge and strengthen the links that connect rural and urban realities. In this quickly changing landscape, rural towns are a significant factor in creating new opportunities, and a flow of goods and services between rural and urban areas is a key part of rural transformation. Our tendency to think in terms of rural-versus-urban will have to evolve into rural-*and*-urban.

In other words, helping rural people like the Dos Santos family achieve their dreams depends on building resilient two-way connections with urban realities and opportunities. At the same time, a strengthened food supply and provision of clean water and other ecosystem services through rural transformation can help urban dwellers achieve their own dreams.

Consider also the case of Peru, where competition and free-market macro-economic policies are working in tandem with socially inclusive rural development policies to create one of the Western Hemisphere's fastest growing and most dynamic economies (Haudry, 2012). This will be the model for 21st-century economic development. At the heart of this model are the small-scale farmers, rural enterprises, and marginalized communities – indigenous peoples, women, and youth – that will make it possible. These are the people that will feed the world tomorrow, protect us from the effects of climate change, and build a sustainable future for our planet.

To support this emerging model, an IFAD-supported project began investing in *yachaq* (lead trainers) who shared their knowledge on farming techniques, soil management, market access, and savings with their *yachacchiqs* (or pupils). These students soon became the teachers, passing on powerful new seeds of knowledge to neighbouring rural communities (ibid.).

The government's investment in rural women has also been central to the country's success. One IFAD-financed project worked with some 9,000 women to open savings accounts. With complementary contributions provided by project funding, these women accrued more than US$1 m in savings (IFAD, 2013c).

Rural transformation is still a work in progress in Peru. Nationally, nearly a third of the population doesn't make enough money to meet basic food needs. Still, its successes to date, and its lessons learned from innovations in social inclusion, could benefit other countries seeking to end rural poverty.

IFAD has a special focus on increasing poor rural people's access to markets – local, peri-urban, urban, and international. Poor rural producers make connections to markets, after all, within larger agricultural value chains. Every product that is sold – locally, nationally, or internationally – is part of a value chain. And every link of the chain has the potential to add value to the product. From a development perspective, value chains are an instrument to harness market forces for the benefit of poor rural women and men – not just producers, but wage earners, service providers, and others.

Agricultural supply chains that span rural and urban areas can offer opportunities for market integration for poor rural producers, notably smallholder family farmers. After all, women and men in rural areas rely predominantly on agriculture. Meanwhile, 2 billion people depend on the world's 500 million smallholder farms for food and income. In many areas, small farms account for as much as 80 per cent of production. Connecting smallholders to markets, enabling them to sell their produce for fair prices and to buy necessary farm inputs – this all helps smallholders build their businesses, increase productivity, and improve their lives and livelihoods.

Despite the continued dominance of agriculture in rural economies, however, 35 to 50 per cent of rural households' income across the developing world does not come from agriculture at all. Instead, it comes from the so-called non-farm economy (Haggblade et al., 2007). This catchall phrase covers a wide range of activities, including agro-processing, trading, manufacturing, and commercial and service enterprises.

IFAD works with partners to build their ability to take part in such activities, which strengthen rural links to the urban world. A key element of this work involves enabling rural people to establish strong producers' organizations, which both increases their bargaining power and helps them to move up the value chain. Such organizations also give the private sector a way to engage with thousands of small producers effectively.

For households with access to land and functioning smallholder farms, additional income earned by family members from other sources makes a huge difference. In fact, rural families with incomes that include non-farm earnings tend to be less poor than those who rely more heavily on agriculture. Non-farm income pays for education and health services, buys agricultural inputs that increase yields, enables smallholders to diversify risk, allows them to invest in their farming businesses, and buys extra food during the hungry season.

The importance of this economy as a source of income and employment for rural people in developing countries is growing everywhere. Increasing the proportion of non-farm income can help families move out of poverty.

IFAD-supported projects foster rural people's ability to earn off-farm income in a variety of ways. Training in entrepreneurship, particularly for young women and men, is a significant activity in many countries. Young people who are able to embrace new technologies and take advantage of new openings can play a vital role in driving rural economic growth. In order to do this, however, they need education and training, as well as access to markets, financial services, and information.

Success will be more likely when rural–urban areas appreciate, and cultivate, their shared interests, especially in light of a changing climate. The bond that cements this partnership might be a shared natural resource base such as a river basin, watershed, or forest area. It could be a corridor that allows goods and services to move between major locations or towards an external market. Or it could be an urban centre that depends on a rural hinterland to provide agricultural goods or protect a fresh water supply (IFAD, 2015f).

One promising area focuses on creating rewards for managing environmental services, a tool that IFAD has already supported in several countries. Upstream farmers, for example, could receive payment for protecting a watershed that generates benefits for downstream water users. In Kenya, for instance, Nairobi depends on the Sasumua dam for 20 per cent of its fresh water, but agricultural activities upstream have negatively impacted water quality and flow. An IFAD-supported pilot project is promoting a rewards-based approach that encourages landowners to adopt sustainable landscape management practices, such as terracing and use of grass waterways (ibid.).

In addition to contributing to rural transformation and strengthening food systems, decent work for young people in rural areas can also help stem urban migration and slow the rising number of slum dwellers. In Africa, for example, more than 60 per cent of the population is currently below the age of 25 (UN Department of Economic and Social Affairs, Population Division, 2015). Decent job opportunities in rural and semirural settings are vital – even under the most optimistic scenarios, urban sectors will not provide enough jobs for all the young women and men who reach working age over the coming decades.

Leveraging remittances

Money sent home in the form of remittances by temporary or permanent migrants makes up another big part of non-farm income. For the period 2013–18, cumulative remittances to developing countries are estimated to surpass US$2.5 tn (IFAD, Financing Facility for Remittances, 2013). Behind these staggering figures lie long days spent working two or three jobs, pleasures forfeited, sacrifices made, years spent living far from the ones they love.

In some recipient countries, remittances are three times greater than official development assistance, and may eventually surpass foreign direct investment (World Bank, Migration and Remittances Team, Development Prospects Group, 2015). In small countries, remittances can be larger than or equal to foreign exchange reserves, also a substantial share of gross domestic product.

In recognition of the growing importance of remittances, IFAD and the World Bank co-host the Global Forum on Remittances every two years. The Forum brings together key stakeholders from the private and public sectors and from civil society to discuss global remittance-related issues. The 2015 Forum, held in Milan, showcased the dynamic and innovative character of European remittance flows, worth almost US$110 bn in 2014. It also highlighted the importance of financial inclusion, the use of innovation and technology to reduce transaction costs, and the importance of diaspora investments for creating employment opportunities back home. The Forum saw the participation of over 400 major stakeholders from the private and public sectors and from civil society. It promoted partnerships, the exchange of knowledge and best practices, and stimulated discussions and debates on global issues related to remittances, migration, and development (IFAD, 2016b).

In 2015, IFAD proclaimed 16 June as the International Day of Family Remittances (IDFR) to recognize the growing importance of migrant workers to rural development in their countries of origin, as well as the economic impact of these workers in their adopted countries. In 2016, the United Nations acknowledged IFAD's initiative, and the role that remittances can play in meeting the challenges facing developing countries, especially in rural areas.

Money from abroad is a lifeline. But while most money sent home is directed to urban areas, the greatest need is in rural areas, where many people in isolated villages are cut off from access to financial services. We need to channel remittances more effectively to create jobs and stimulate local economies, including more investment in the agricultural sector.

Most remittances are used for basic goods such as food, clothing, shelter, medicine, and education. However, studies indicate that globally about US$80 bn –about 20 per cent of remittances – could be available for investments if migrant workers and receiving families had more options to use their funds. Of that amount, about US$34 bn would be available in rural areas (IFAD Newsroom, 2015).

To that end, IFAD manages the multi-donor Financing Facility for Remittances (FFR) to help ensure that even the most isolated rural clients could access remittances and related financial services. The FFR, created in 2006, works with public, private, and civil society partners. Among its goals, it supports innovative approaches to reducing the cost of remittances and empowering migrant workers and their families to use their funds to improve their livelihoods and those of their communities (IFAD, 2013e).

In one partnership supported by the FFR, for example, the International Agency for Source Country Information (IASCI) worked with commercial banks to mobilize migrant capital in Albania and Kosovo. The project created migrant-tailored financial products that promote higher returns, increase migrant earnings, and attract migrant savings to the country of origin. In Albania and Kosovo, over 1,100 migrants made use of the new products (ibid.).

IFAD's experience shows that investing in rural people is a viable business proposition. If we empower people to fund their own development, they can raise their income, create jobs, and generate environmental and social benefits. But many barriers still prevent the use of remittances as an investment tool in rural areas.

While the average cost of sending money home has declined in recent years, it is still too high (World Bank, 2015). In parts of Africa, costs can be above 12 per cent. Reducing these costs to 3 per cent would put more than US$20 bn annually in the pockets of migrants and their relatives (De, 2015).

How can we reduce these costs?

Post offices are a largely untapped resource for managing remittances. In West Africa, in collaboration with the Universal Postal Union (UPU), an IFAD-funded project enabled 355 rural post offices to offer electronic money transfers. It cut the cost of remittances in half, and reduced transfer times from two weeks to two days. We began scaling up this approach in Central and Southeast Asia, holding the promise of cheaper and faster financial services for millions of people (IFAD, 2013d).

Bringing services to the people is another key challenge. In remote and rural areas, many people must walk for kilometres to reach the closest receiving point. Then, loaded with cash, they must risk the journey home again. In Pakistan, EasyPaisa uses mobile phones to bring financial services to people rather than forcing them to reach financial service providers (Remittances Gateway, 2014). This eliminates high cost structure that makes traditional rural financial services so expensive.

But the most formidable barrier of all is lack of access to basic financial services. Without accessible financial services, such as credit, savings, and insurance, small producers and micro-entrepreneurs struggle to pay for basic inputs or equipment that would enable them to boost productivity, build their businesses, and connect to markets.

IFAD continues to address these challenges with its national, international, and local partners. For their part, governments can make sure family farms are connected to markets, with roads, power, cold storage, and access to seeds and fertilizers. With these connections, smallholder farmers can use remittances to raise productivity. Often, lack of money is not the problem. Rather, what's missing are lack of good opportunities and enabling investment mechanisms.

Remittances and diaspora savings are not a magic formula. And they are not a substitute for ODA or other private sources of funding for development. But they are a rich resource of non-farm income for millions of families who are trying to follow their dreams – if we can empower them to harness the funds effectively.

New options for rural people

Studies have shown that rural towns are effective generators of non-farm employment as they mediate the flow of inputs, goods, and services between more isolated rural areas and larger urban centres (Haggblade et al., 2007). These small towns can become a focus for the diversification of rural economies. These diversified economies are still based on agricultural production, but they connect farmers to other key actors along value chains, including processors and traders.

There is also evidence that rural non-farm diversification and the growth of small towns can reduce poverty faster than rapid growth in large cities. A 15-year study by the World Bank in rural Tanzania shows the importance of the non-farm economy. It showed that six out of seven people who escaped poverty were either farmers who supplemented their incomes with non-farm earnings or people who moved out of farming into the non-farm rural sector. Only one in seven people who moved out of poverty did so by migrating to big cities (Christiaensen et al., 2013).

Non-farm income can be particularly vital to two vulnerable groups, namely landless people and women. Rural families with little or no secure access to land earn between 30 and 90 per cent of their income from non-farm activities (Haggblade et al., 2010). And women in rural areas often earn small but precious amounts of cash from household-based microenterprises.

This is especially important in places where their movements are restricted by traditional norms, and their heavy domestic workload leaves them little time or energy to devote to earning extra income outside the home. A heavy workload is a daily fact of life for huge numbers of women. As I noted in Chapter 5, UN Women's *Progress of the World's Women* in 2015 reported that women typically spend two and a half times as long as men on unpaid care work, mostly tending to children and the elderly.

With the non-farm rural economy providing up to half of rural income in developing countries, policymakers sometimes regard the sector as an alternative to agriculture to drive economic growth outside urban areas (Haggblade et al., 2007). However, the farm and non-farm economies are both fundamental to the twin development goals of poverty reduction and food security. Under the right conditions, growth in one feeds growth in the other in a virtuous circle.

At the level of rural households where income derives from both sectors, the synergies are clear, particularly where non-farm income is invested in family farming businesses. At the level of the local economy, smallholders who are making bigger profits have more money to spend in local businesses and service providers. A more economically vibrant rural community will generate stronger demand in turn for local agricultural produce, stimulating farmers to increase and diversify production.

However, inclusive growth in the farm and non-farm sectors of the rural economy can only take place when basic key conditions are met. Rural infrastructure – particularly roads, transport, and markets, must be adequate and accessible to everyone. Essential services – including health, education, and financial services – must be available. Rural areas must be interconnected both physically and digitally with urban areas.

Unfortunately, in many rural areas of developing countries the necessary infrastructure is not yet in place. For example, although there is a strong positive correlation between economic development and the quality of road networks, lack of infrastructure can isolate rural people or oblige them to engage in urban markets and value chains on very unequal terms.

As the *2014 Africa Progress Report* points out, no region has fewer developed road networks and energy systems than Africa. It estimates the cost of filling the gaps in basic infrastructure in Africa at around US$48 bn (Africa Progress Panel, 2014). Given the huge investment required, regional cooperation on energy and transport is vital to achieve economies of scale in infrastructure projects. Such investments, however, will not necessarily overcome the financial exclusion experienced by isolated and vulnerable populations. To tackle the issue of rural poverty at its roots and to strengthen local and national food systems, governments and partners must invest in the economic and social transformation of rural areas. This means developing smallholder agriculture, fostering the non-farm sector, investing in rural infrastructure and services, facilitating private sector investment, and connecting rural people to urban and peri-urban markets and opportunities.

Information and communications technologies generally, and mobile telephones in particular, are playing a rapidly growing role in connecting people of all ages along the rural–urban continuum with information and services. Today, even in remote areas, increasing numbers of women and men own or are able to access a phone.

Growth in mobile use is particularly strong in Africa, Asia and the Pacific, where penetration rates reached 69 and 89 per cent in 2014 (ITU, 2014). Mobile money transfer services are now widely available in developing countries, making it faster, cheaper, and safer to move money.

There is also a whole range of short message service (or SMS)-based services available to smallholder farmers, offering information on seed pricing, weather forecasts, pest outbreaks, market prices, and more. It's no exaggeration to say that a mobile phone can be a world of opportunities in the palm of your hand.

The success of the global community's renewed efforts to eradicate hunger and poverty – and to strengthen food systems to the benefit of producers and consumers –will depend in no small part on governments, donors, and the private sector working together to build resilient links between remote settlements, villages, small towns, urban centres, and megacities. These links must include hard infrastructure and virtual connectivity. Both are essential to ensure the two-way flow of goods, resources, information, and labour and to make the rural–urban divide truly a thing of the past.

Financing for development

With the endorsement of the SDGs, the world has renewed its commitment to ending hunger and poverty. But even with the best of intentions, commitments alone will not feed people or create prosperity. Without accompanying financing, the dream of achieving the SDGs by 2030 will remain unfulfilled.

Official development assistance remains an important source of funding, but on its own it will not be enough. For some time, IFAD has been exploring new avenues of financing for development. Most recently, our Sovereign Borrowing Framework has provided the means to leverage additional resources and manage them more flexibly. It has already resulted in a financing agreement with the KfW Development Bank of Germany (IFAD, 2015h). We have also developed a framework for Reimbursable Technical Assistance (RTA), which is a more knowledge-oriented way of working with IFAD; it provides aid in the form of technical assistance rather than pure funding, particularly for middle-income countries (IFAD, 2012c).

In response to the present migration crisis, IFAD is also creating a Facility for Refugees, Migrants, Forced Displacement and Rural Stability (FARMS) (IFAD, 2016a). The Facility aims to build on IFAD's existing investment portfolio to finance targeted and more inclusive interventions before, during, and after periods of displacement and increased migration. This will provide a motivation to return home for people who have left, and a chance for a life of dignity and opportunity for those who remain. With a targeted envelope of US$100 m, FARMS will initially address the needs of affected communities in the Near East and North Africa region, where the crisis is most severe.

Because resources are finite, we also have to do better in gathering hard evidence of the results of our work. IFAD is leading the development community in establishing a scientific approach to impact assessment that looks not just at this or that project, but the effectiveness of the institution as a whole and its impact on rural lives.

This is not to say we have all the answers; rather, it is an illustration that no institution can stop moving in a changing world. We cannot let the pace of change outrun us, or we will pay the cost of inaction once again. IFAD is based on partnership, and it is committed to sharing whatever knowledge it generates with the world. Building a sustainable future is a collective enterprise. Our destinies are both individual and collective at the same time.

Agriculture is now highly visible on the global agenda. This is only right, because we depend on it for our lives. The issues that deeply affect smallholder farmers and other rural people are also beginning to get the attention that they deserve – not just in dialogues, but in policies and concrete investments. We must maintain this commitment and increase our awareness of the vital importance of the rural space. If we do so, I believe that we will stand a much better chance of achieving the 2030 Agenda, because a universal agenda demands a holistic vision. We live in an interconnected world. If we achieve a sustainable future, it will be because we worked together to reach the stream.

It's all about the people

Resources, inputs, knowledge, infrastructure, policies, finance – there are many key components of inclusive rural transformation. But in the end, it is the people who matter. Unless we put women and men at the centre of our vision for development, and unless there are leaders that inspire, and give courage and hope, little progress will be made toward the SDGs and the 2030 Agenda.

I have cited the example of three communities I visited in Ethiopia, where two were moving ahead and one had yet to make a real start. Two were practicing participatory, people-centred development, with innovation, change, and learning, while the third was stuck in non-inclusive patterns and practices.

Money and tools are not enough; it matters whose hands you put them in, who the leaders are, and how everyone plays their part. Similarly, science and technology are not magical solutions that produce development; they are ingredients that can lead to amazing transformations when used wisely, inclusively, and with the full participation of the people concerned.

Instead of three communities we could choose three countries, and find the pattern replicated. Some have been stuck in cycles of conflict, poor leadership, corruption, and under-investment that have left the people hungry and the countries unstable for years or even decades. But there are others that have fulfilled their commitments, invested in agriculture, created an enabling environment, and done much to improve the livelihoods of rural people, as well as to strengthen the national economy and food security.

And then there is our world, our planet – the ultimate boundary for all the challenges that we face and all the hopes that we treasure. There are now more than 7 billion people on earth and issues like climate change, conflict, forced migration, and inequality affect every one of us. This means that the solutions to those challenges must also be owned not only by leaders but by us all. As the 2030 Agenda states, we need to make our goals universal and our actions inclusive. For me, and for IFAD, that means extending our reach to the world's most forgotten people. Inclusive, sustainable development is a moral and generational imperative.

References

Adejumobi, S. and Olukoshi, A. (2008) *The African Union and New Strategies for Development in Africa*, Cambria Press, Amherst.

Adhikari, B. and Rambaran, Y. (2012) 'CURE shares knowledge in Nepal's Western Uplands through TIS', IFAD Asia [website] <http://asia.ifad.org/web/drought/home?p_p_id=1_WAR_ifad_newsportlet&_1_WAR_ifad_newsportlet_jspPage=%2Fview_entry.jsp&_1_WAR_ifad_newsportlet_entryId=4412> (posted 2 May 2012) [accessed 7 October 2016].

Africa Progress Panel (2014) *Grain fish money: Financing Africa's Green and Blue Revolutions*, Africa Progress Report [online]. Africa Progress Panel, Geneva. Available from: http://www.afdb.org/fileadmin/uploads/afdb/Documents/Project-and-Operations/Africa_Progress_Report_2014.PDF [accessed 10 October 2016].

Africa Progress Panel (2015) *Power People Planet: Seizing Africa's Energy and Climate Opportunities*, Africa Progress Report [online]. Africa Progress Panel, Geneva. Available from: http://www.africaprogresspanel.org/wp-content/uploads/2015/06/APP_REPORT_2015_FINAL_low1.pdf [accessed 7 October 2016].

African Development Bank Group, Organisation for Economic Co-operation and Development (OECD), United Nations Development Programme (UNDP), and United Nations Economic Commission for Africa (2012) *African Economic*

Outlook 2012: Promoting Youth Employment [online]. OECD, Paris <http://dx.doi.org/10.1787/aeo-2012-en>.

African Development Bank Group (2012) 'Urbanization in Africa' [blog], AfDB, <http://www.afdb.org/en/blogs/afdb-championing-inclusive-growth-across-africa/post/urbanization-in-africa-10143/> (posted 13 December 2012) [accessed 7 October 2016].

Agbor, J., Taiwo, O. and Smith, J. (2012) 'Sub-Saharan Africa's youth bulge: A demographic dividend or disaster?' In: *Foresight Africa Top Priorities for the Continent in 2012* [online]. African Growth Initiative at Brookings, Washington, DC. Available from: https://www.brookings.edu/wp-content/uploads/2016/06/01_foresight_africa_full_report.pdf [accessed 10 October 2016].

Agricultural Innovation MKTPlace (n.d.) 'Agricultural Innovation MKTPlace' [website] <http://www.mktplace.org/site/images/folder1.pdf> [accessed 3 October 2016].

Aryal, J.P., Sapkota, T.B., Jat, M.L. and Bishnoi, D.K. (2015) 'On-farm economic and environmental impact of zero-tillage wheat: A case of North-West India', *Experimental Agriculture 51*, no. 01 (2015), 1–16 <http://dx.doi.org/10.1017/S001447971400012X>.

Auty, R.M. (2001) 'Introduction and Overview', in: Auty, R.M. (ed.) *Resource Abundance and Economic Development*, Oxford University Press, pp. 3–16.

Babcock, L.H. (2015) *Mobile Payments: How Digital Finance Is Transforming Agriculture*, Value Chains & Trade [online]. Technical Centre for Agricultural and Rural Cooperation, The Netherlands. Available from: http://publications.cta.int/media/publications/downloads/1849_PDF.pdf/ [accessed 7 October 2016].

Beavogui, M. (2010) 'FIDAction in West and Central Africa', [website] October 2010, <https://www.ifad.org/newsletter/pa/e/18_full.htm> [accessed 10 October 2016].

Beegle, K., Christiaensen, L., Dabalen, A. and Gaddis, I. (2016) *Poverty in a Rising Africa* [online]. World Bank

Publications, Washington, DC <http://dx.doi.org/10.1596/978-1-4648-0723-7>.

Benchwick, G. (2010) 'Innovation Marketplace' provides knowledge sharing forum for Africa and Brazil' [blog] IFAD Social Reporting Blog <http://ifad-un.blogspot.it/2010/05/innovation-marketplace-provides.html> (posted 11 May 2010) [accessed 10 October 2016].

Borlaug, N. (1970) 'Acceptance Speech' [website] Nobel Prize <http://www.nobelprize.org/nobel_prizes/peace/laureates/1970/borlaug-acceptance.html> [accessed 10 October 2016].

Burke, M.B., Miguel, E., Satyanath, S., Dykema, J.A. and Lobell, D.B. (2009) 'Warming increases the risk of civil war in Africa', *Proceedings of the National Academy of Sciences*, 106(49), pp. 20670–74.

Center for Evaluation (2012) *Final evaluation of "SCAMPIS" – Scaling up micro-irrigation systems in India, Madagascar and Guatemala* [online] Center for Evaluation, Saarbrücken. Available from: https://www.ifad.org/documents/10180/dd447de6-a427-45cd-a88f-06527e4d6f86 [accessed 10 October 2016].

CGAP (n.d.) 'Digital financial services' [website] <https://www.cgap.org/topics/digital-financial-services> [accessed 8 September 2016].

CGIAR (n.d.) 'Cassava' [website] <http://www.cgiar.org/our-strategy/crop-factsheets/cassava/> [accessed 30 September 2016].

Chhattisgarh Tribal Development Programme (n.d.) 'Chhattisgarh Tribal Development Programme', Loan No-506IN <http://cjtdp.nic.in/Proj_summary_E.htm> (posted 7 September 2016) [accessed 6 October 2016].

Christiaensen, L. and Demery, L. (2007) *Down to Earth: Agriculture and Poverty Reduction in Africa*, World Bank Publications, Washington, DC <http://dx.doi.org/ 10.1596/978-0-8213-6854-1>.

Christiaensen, L., De Weerdt, J. and Todo, Y. (2013) *Urbanization and Poverty Reduction: The Role of Rural Diversification and Secondary Towns*, Policy Research Working Paper 6422 [online]. World Bank, Washington, DC. Available from: http://dx.doi.org/10.1596/1813-9450-6422 [accessed 10 October 2016].

Committee on World Food Security (2014) *Principles for Responsible Investment in Agriculture and Food Systems* [online]. IFAD, Rome. Available from: http://www.fao.org/fileadmin/templates/cfs/Docs1314/rai/CFS_Principles_Oct_2014_EN.pdf [accessed 10 October 2016].

Cooper, P.J.M., Cappiello S., Vermeulen, S.J., Campbell, B.M., Zougmoré, R. and Kinyangi, J. (2013) 'Large-scale implementation of adaptation and mitigation actions in agriculture', Working Paper 50 [online]. CGIAR Research Programme on Climate Change, Agriculture and Food Security, Denmark. Available from: https://cgspace.cgiar.org/rest/bitstreams/24708/retrieve [accessed 7 October 2016].

Dabla-Norris, E., Kochhar, K., Ricka, F., Suphaphiphat, N. and Tsounta, E. (2015) *Causes and Consequences of Income Inequality: A Global Perspective*, IMF Staff Discussion Note [online]. International Monetary Fund, Washington, DC. Available from: https://www.imf.org/external/pubs/ft/sdn/2015/sdn1513.pdf [accessed 7 October 2016].

Das, S. 'How the cost of Ebola damaged the entire African economy' *The Independent* [website] <http://www.independent.co.uk/voices/how-the-cost-of-ebola-damaged-the-entire-african-economy-a6965081.html> (posted 2 April 2016) [accessed 10 October 2016].

De, S. (2015) 'Reducing remittance costs and the financing for development strategy' [blog] People Move <http://blogs.worldbank.org/peoplemove/reducing-remittance-costs-and-

financing-development-strategy> (posted 18 December 2015) [accessed 10 October 2016].

Donnelly, J. *Passion Beyond Normal: How Farmers and Researchers Are Finding Solutions to Africa's Hunger* [online]. CGIAR, Washington, DC. Available from: http://documents.worldbank.org/curated/en/751901468009599575/pdf/634110WP0Passi00Box0361517B0PUBLIC0.pdf [accessed 10 October 2016].

ECLAC (2014) 'Foreign Trade in Latin America and the Caribbean' [website] <http://www.cepal.org/en/infographics/foreign-trade-latin-america-and-caribbean> (posted 24 November 2014) [accessed 10 October 2016].

The Economist (2011) 'Africa's impressive growth' [website] <http://www.economist.com/blogs/dailychart/2011/01/daily_chart> (posted 6 January 2011) [accessed 10 October 2016].

Edwards, A. (2016) 'Global forced displacement hits record high' [website] UNHCR News <http://www.unhcr.org/news/latest/2016/6/5763b65a4/global-forced-displacement-hits-record-high.html> (posted 20 June 2016) [accessed 6 October 2016].

Ethiopian Agricultural Transformation Agency (n.d.) 'EthioSIS' [website] <http://www.ata.gov.et/highlighted-deliverables/ethiosis/> [accessed 10 October 2016].

Extractive Industries Transparency Initiative (EITI) (2016) *2016 Progress Report: From Reports to Results* [online]. EITI: Oslo. Available from: https://eiti.org/files/progressreport.pdf [accessed 10 October 2016].

FAO (2002) *The State of Food Insecurity in the World 2002* [online]. FAO, Rome. Available from: http://www.fao.org/docrep/005/y7352e/y7352e00.HTM [accessed 10 October 2016].

FAO (2005) *Irrigation in Africa in Figures: AQUASTAT Survey – 2005*, FAO Water Reports 29 [online]. FAO, Rome. Available from: ftp://ftp.fao.org/agl/aglw/docs/wr29_eng.pdf [accessed 6 October 2016].

FAO (2008), *State of Food Insecurity in the World 2008: High Food Prices and Food Security – Threats and Opportunities* [online]. FAO, Rome. Available from: *State of Food Insecurity in the World 2008* [accessed 10 October 2016].

FAO (2011a) *Global Food Losses and Food Waste: Extent, Causes, and Prevention* [online]. FAO, Rome. Available from: http://www.fao.org/docrep/014/mb060e/mb060e.pdf [accessed 6 October 2016].

FAO (2011b) *The State of Food and Agriculture 2010–2011: Women in Agriculture, Closing the Gender Gap for Development* [online]. FAO, Rome. Available from: http://www.fao.org/docrep/013/i2050e/i2050e.pdf [accessed 10 October 2016].

FAO (2012a) *FAO Statistical Yearbook 2012: World Food and Agriculture* [online.] FAO, Rome. Available from: http://reliefweb.int/sites/reliefweb.int/files/resources/i2490e.pdf [accessed 10 October 2016].

FAO (2012b) 'Smallholders and family farmers', Sustainability Pathways [online]. FAO, Rome. Available from: http://www.fao.org/fileadmin/templates/nr/sustainability_pathways/docs/Factsheet_SMALLHOLDERS.pdf [accessed 7 October 2016].

FAO (2012c), *Towards the Future we Want: End Hunger and Make the Transition to Sustainable Agricultural and Food Systems* [online]. FAO, Rome. Available from: http://www.fao.org/docrep/015/an894e/an894e00.pdf [accessed 7 October 2016].

FAO (2014) 'Food security for sustainable development and urbanization: Inputs for FAO's contribution to the 2014 ECOSOC Integration Segment, 27–29 May', Contribution to the 2014 United Nations Economic and Social Council (ECOSOC) Integration Segment [online]. FAO, Rome 2014.

Available from: http://www.un.org/en/ecosoc/integration/pdf/foodandagricultureorganization.pdf [accessed 7 October 2016].

FAO (2016a) 'Countries requiring external assistance for food' [website] <http://www.fao.org/GIEWS/ENGLISH/hotspots/index.htm> (posted September 2016) [accessed 10 October 2016].

FAO (2016b), 'How to Feed the World in 2050' [pdf] <http://www.fao.org/fileadmin/templates/wsfs/docs/expert_paper/How_to_Feed_the_World_in_2050.pdf> [accessed 8 September 2016].

FAO (2016) 'Why gender ::: Key facts' [website] <http://www.fao.org/gender/gender-home/gender-why/key-facts/en/> [accessed 16 September 2016].

FAO (n.d. a) 'Background' [website] <http://www.fao.org/in-action/action-against-desertification/background/en/> [accessed 9 September 2016].

FAO (n.d. b) 'Climate-smart agriculture' [website] <http://www.fao.org/climate-smart-agriculture/en> [accessed 9 September, 2016].

FAO Emergencies (2016), 'Ebola outbreak in West Africa' [website] <http://www.fao.org/emergencies/crisis/ebola/intro/en/> [accessed 19 September 2016].

FAO News (2012) 'Countries adopt global guidelines on tenure of land, forests, fisheries' [website] <http://www.fao.org/news/story/en/item/142587/icode/> (posted 11 May 2012) [accessed 10 October 2016].

FAO, IFAD, and WFP (2012) *The State of Food Insecurity in the World 2012: Economic Growth is Necessary but not Sufficient to Accelerate Reduction of Hunger and Malnutrition* [online]. FAO, Rome. Available from: http://www.fao.org/docrep/016/i3027e/i3027e.pdf [accessed 10 October 2016].

FAO, IFAD, and WFP (2015) *The State of Food Insecurity in the World 2015: Meeting the 2015 International Hunger Targets: Taking Stock of Uneven Progress* [online]. FAO, Rome.

Available from: http://www.fao.org/3/a4ef2d16-70a7-460a-a9ac-2a65a533269a/i4646e.pdf [accessed 6 October 2016].

FARA (2014) *Science Agenda for Agriculture in Africa: 'Connecting Science' to Transform Agriculture in Africa* [online]. FARA, Accra. Available from: http://faraafrica.org/wp-content/uploads/2015/04/English_Science_agenda_for_agr_in_Africa.pdf [accessed 10 October 2016].

Global Youth Innovation Network (n.d.) 'What is GYIN?' [website] <http://www.gyin.org/about-us/what-is-gyin/> [accessed 15 September 2016].

Goedde, L., Horii, M. and Sanghvi, S (2015) 'Pursuing the global opportunity in food and agribusiness' [website], McKinsey & Company. <http://www.mckinsey.com/industries/chemicals/our-insights/pursuing-the-global-opportunity-in-food-and-agribusiness> [blog] (posted July 2015) [accessed 7 October 2016].

GSMA Intelligence (2015) Case study: Vodafone Turkey Farmers' Club [online]. GSMA. Available from: http://www.gsma.com/mobilefordevelopment/wp-content/uploads/2015/06/GSMA_Case_VodafoneTurkey_18Aug2015.pdf [accessed 11 January 2017].

Haggblade, S., Hazell, P.B.R. and Reardon, T. (2010) 'The rural non-farm economy: Prospects for growth and poverty reduction', *World Development* 38, no. 10 (2010): 1429–41. <http://dx.doi.org/10.1016/j.worlddev.2009.06.008>.

Haggblade, S., Hazell, P.B.R. and Reardon, T. (eds) (2007) *Transforming the Rural Nonfarm Economy: Opportunities and Threats in the Developing World* [online]. IFPRI, Washington, DC. Available from: http://ebrary.ifpri.org/cdm/ref/collection/p15738coll2/id/126215 [accessed 10 October 2016].

Hallegatte, S., Bangalore, M., Bonzanigo, L., Fay, M., Kane, T., Narloch, U., Rozenberg, J., Treguer, D. and Vogt-Schlib, A. (2015) *Shock Waves: Managing the Impacts of Climate Change on Poverty*, Climate Change and Development Series, World

Bank, Washington, DC. Available from: http://dx.doi.org/10.1596/978-1-4648-0673-5 [accessed 6 October 2016].

Haudry, R. (2012) 'Peru is a leader for innovative models of socially inclusive rural development', in *Rural Perspectives: Sharing Experiences from Latin America and the Caribbean*, 10 [website] <https://www.ifad.org/newsletter/pl/e/10_full.htm#3> [accessed 10 October 2016].

HLPE (2013) *Investing in Smallholder Agriculture for Food Security* [online]. HLPE, Rome. Available from: http://www.fao.org/fileadmin/user_upload/hlpe/hlpe_documents/HLPE_Reports/HLPE-Report-6_Investing_in_smallholder_agriculture.pdf [accessed 6 October 2016].

Hoddinott, J. and Haddad, L. (1995) 'Does female income share influence household expenditures? Evidence from Côte D'Ivoire', *Oxford Bulletin of Economic and Statistics* 57 (1995): pp. 77–96.

Horton, R. and Lo, S. 'Nutrition: a quintessential sustainable development goal', *The Lancet* 382, no. 9890 (2013): 371–72 <http://dx.doi.org/10.1016/ S0140-6736(13)61100-9>.

ICRISAT (2001) 'SATrends Issue 2' [website] <http://www.icrisat.org/what-we-do/satrends/01jan/1.htm> [accessed 10 October 2016].

IDMC (2013) *Global Estimates 2012: People Displaced by Disasters* [online]. IDMC, Geneva. Available from: http://www.internal-displacement.org/assets/publications/2013/2012-global-estimates-corporate-en.pdf [accessed 7 October 2016].

IDMC (2015) 'Global estimates 2015: People displaced by disasters' [pdf] <http://www.internal-displacement.org/assets/library/Media/201507-globalEstimates-2015/GE-2015-HighlightsFINAL.pdf> [accessed 7 October 2016].

IFAD (2011a) 'Higher and volatile food prices and poor rural people' [online]. Rome, IFAD. Available from: https://www.ifad.org/documents/10180/a0e7d3d6-084a-48a1-b358-13a76b7b62b2 [accessed 10 October 2016].

IFAD (2011b) 'President's report: Proposed grant to the Democratic Republic of Timor-Leste for the Timor-Leste Maize Storage Project', EB 2011/104/R.25/Rev.1 [online]. IFAD, Rome. Available from: https://webapps.ifad.org/members/eb/104/docs/EB-2011-104-R-25-Rev-1.pdf [accessed 7 October 2016].

IFAD (2011c) 'Regreening the Sahel: Developing agriculture in the context of climate change in Burkina Faso', Information Sheet: West and Central Africa [online]. IFAD, Rome. Available from: https://www.ifad.org/documents/10180/5e333813-f355-4144-8a78-6fef533c775f [accessed 10 October 2016].

IFAD (2011d) 'Republic of India: Country strategic opportunities programme', EB 2011/102/R.13 [pdf] <https://www.ifad.org/documents/10180/8df661cd-39f5-4adb-8ba9-8335595a1a59> [accessed 7 October 2016].

IFAD (2011e) 'South–South cooperation in IFAD's business model' REPL. IX/3/R.3 [pdf] <https://www.ifad.org/documents/10180/5daaf5d9-1908-420f-a4bc-6d627e99e9a9> [accessed 10 October 2016].

IFAD (2012a) *Access to Markets: Making Value Chains Work for Poor Rural People* [online]. IFAD, Rome. Available from: https://www.ifad.org/documents/10180/650e771a-ef4a-4893-967b-2d5fd8eef313 [accessed 7 October 2016].

IFAD (2012b) 'Gender equality and women's empowerment', Fact Sheet [online]. IFAD, Rome. Available from: https://www.ifad.org/documents/10180/5bcb54e2-96d1-4e95-932b-d7ad9761f972 [accessed 7 October 2016].

IFAD (2012c) 'Instrument establishing the Reimbursable Technical Assistance (RTA) Programme', EB 2012/105/R.28 [pdf] <https://webapps.ifad.org/members/eb/105/docs/EB-2012-105-R-28.pdf> [accessed 10 October 2016].

IFAD (2012d) 'Land tenure security and poverty reduction' [online]. IFAD, Rome. Available from: https://www.ifad.org/

documents/10180/0f715abf-3f59-41f6-ac08-28403ebd271f [accessed 10 October 2016].

IFAD (2012e) *Smallholders Fulfil Their Households' Needs With a New Way of Farming Rice*, East and Southern Africa: Seeds of Innovation [online]. IFAD, Rome. Available from: https://www.ifad.org/documents/10180/9f8c4ad4-c6cb-45de-af26-e6cfe611def2 [accessed 10 October 2016].

IFAD (2013a) *Annual Report 2013* [online.]IFAD, Rome. Available from: https://www.ifad.org/documents/10180/40dbb482-581a-4123-be7e-bc0acb1ba956 [accessed 7 October 2016].

IFAD (2013b) *Country-Level Policy Engagement: Opportunity and Necessity* [online]. IFAD, Rome. Available from: https://www.ifad.org/documents/10180/2f7ad2b7-e833-412a-aba3-8c0c94f2d99a [accessed 10 October 2016].

IFAD (2013c) *Enabling Poor Rural People to Overcome Poverty in Peru* [online]. IFAD, Rome. Available from: https://www.ifad.org/documents/10180/f81cc4d3-14ac-412f-9b2a-9701b2fa6a14 [accessed 10 October 2016].

IFAD (2013d) *The FFR Brief: Five years of the Financing Facility for Remittances and the road ahead* [online]. IFAD, Rome. Available from: https://www.ifad.org/documents/10180/e5b2381d-52dc-43c6-a95b-02fa8423d6e5 [accessed 10 October 2016].

IFAD (2013e) *Financing Facility for Remittances* [online]. IFAD, Rome. Available from: https://www.ifad.org/documents/10180/63cc53e1-992a-4d0f-9485-05ef006d3e19 [accessed 10 October 2016].

IFAD (2013f) 'Mainstreaming Policy dialogue: From vision to action', Workshop report [online]. IFAD, Rome. Available from: https://www.ifad.org/documents/10180/e165754e-b404-4023-84f7-6930a24238a5 [accessed 10 October 2016].

IFAD (2013g) *Smallholders, Food Security, and the Environment* [online]. IFAD, Rome. Available from: https://www.ifad.org/

documents/10180/666cac24-14b6-43c2-876d-9c2d1f01d5dd [accessed 6 October 2016].

IFAD (2013h) *Small-Scale Producers in the Development of Cocoa Value-Chain Partnerships* [online]. IFAD, Rome. Available from: https://www.ifad.org/documents/10180/b8249b3d-7733-4f4b-951c-a80aa6d8619e [accessed 7 October 2016].

IFAD (2013i) *Support to Farmers' Organizations in Africa Programme (SFOAP) : Main Phase (2013-2017)* [online]. IFAD, Rome. Available from: https://www.ifad.org/documents/10180/848cdae8-3c5e-4a0e-8538-e7333e2b75ea [accessed 7 October 2016].

IFAD (2014a) *Fulfilling the Promise of African Agriculture: IFAD in Africa* [online]. IFAD, Rome. Available from: https://www.ifad.org/documents/10180/cb0aad9b-c24a-44cc-a321-4ce48f01953d [accessed 7 October 2016].

IFAD (2014b) *Household Methodologies: Harnessing the Family's Potential for Change*, Gender, targeting and social inclusion [online]. IFAD, Rome. Available from: https://www.ifad.org/documents/10180/c89c54a6-fb41-4df0-9bf8-ef6ff4e4bc9a [accessed 7 October 2016].

IFAD (2014c) *Improving Nutrition Through Agriculture* [online]. IFAD, Rome. Available from: https://www.ifad.org/documents/10180/a986d248-ad22-4ea5-81e1-e7d7daa3ebd4 [accessed 10 October 2016].

IFAD (2014d) *Investing in Rural People in the United Republic of Tanzania: Rural Poverty in the United Republic of Tanzania* [online]. IFAD, Rome. Available from: https://www.ifad.org/documents/10180/feb514f1-a0d2-4111-8d98-50be8ddd0184 [accessed 10 October 2016].

IFAD (2014e) *Investing in Smallholder Family Farmers… For the Future We Want*, 2014 Governing Council [online]. IFAD, Rome. Available from: https://www.ifad.org/documents/10180/f484c453-e248-483c-871b-b0acb14bf894 [accessed 7 October 2016].

IFAD (2014f) *Youth: Investing in Young Rural People for Sustainable and Equitable Development* [online]. IFAD, Rome. Available from: https://www.ifad.org/documents/10180/15b7d693-89b0-4c5d-ae50-80ad0d74b898 [accessed 7 October 2016].

IFAD (2015a) *Annual Report 2015* [online]. IFAD, Rome. Available from: https://www.ifad.org/documents/10180/a1b08710-57c8-40fe-878d-c598a96f0d95 [accessed 10 October 2016].

IFAD (2015b) *Climate Change and Food Security: Innovations for Smallholder Agriculture* [online]. IFAD, Rome. Available from: https://www.ifad.org/documents/10180/4fd1ef2d-c936-4134-a443-3e686a3bdc8e [accessed 7 October 2016].

IFAD (2015c) *Finance for Food: Investing in Agriculture for a Sustainable Future* [online]. IFAD, Rome. Available from: https://www.ifad.org/documents/10180/19e44376-0328-4008-829e-8196d3d2ab27 [accessed 7 October 2016].

IFAD (2015d) 'IFAD submission to UNFCCC Lima Work Programme on Gender and Workshop during the 42nd session of the Subsidiary Body for Implementation (June 2015)' [pdf] <https://unfccc.int/files/documentation/submissions_from_non-party_stakeholders/application/pdf/505.pdf> [accessed 10 October 2016].

IFAD (2015e) *Land Tenure Security*, Scaling up note [online]. IFAD, Rome. Available from https://www.ifad.org/documents/10180/2606bb19-45dc-45af-8a38-a6bcfbcaec87 [accessed 10 October 2016].

IFAD (2015f) *Leveraging the rural-urban nexus for development* IFAD Post-2015 Policy brief 1 [online]. IFAD, Rome. Available from: https://www.ifad.org/documents/10180/1067913d-6bec-4057-9ca9-23bc2fefe910 [accessed 10 October 2016].

IFAD (2015g) *Nigeria*, Scaling up note [online]. IFAD, Rome. Available from: https://www.ifad.org/documents/10180/359371f0-9c0c-4d07-a87b-49df00c6e66d [accessed 7 October 2016].

IFAD (2015h) 'Sovereign borrowing framework: Borrowing from sovereign states and state-supported institutions' EB 2015/114/R.17/Rev.1 [pdf] <https://webapps.ifad.org/members/eb/114/docs/EB-2015-114-R-17-Rev-1.pdf> [accessed 10 October 2016].

IFAD (2016a) 'Facility for Refugees, Migrants, Forced Displacement and Rural Stability (FARMS)', EB 2016/118/INF.6 [pdf] <https://webapps.ifad.org/members/eb/118/docs/EB-2016-118-INF-6.pdf> [accessed 10 October 2016].

IFAD (2016b) *Global Forum on Remittances and Development 2015: Official Report* [online]. IFAD, Rome. Available from: https://www.ifad.org/documents/10180/219b188b-7b79-4bf1-af00-003d90ba29d6 [accessed 10 October 2016].

IFAD (2016c) *Rural Development Report 2016: Fostering Inclusive Rural Transformation* [online]. IFAD, Rome. Available from: https://www.ifad.org/documents/30600024/30604583/RDR_WEB.pdf/c734d0c4-fbb1-4507-9b4b-6c432c6f38c3 [accessed 6 October 2016].

IFAD (n. d. a) *Empowering the Poor by Shifting from a Supply to a Demand-Driven Approach*, Case Study – Peru [online]. IFAD, Rome. Available from: https://www.ifad.org/documents/10180/b4ac8fa2-5463-4b97-9842-8596bb6b5a83 [accessed 7 October 2016].

IFAD (n.d. b) 'Inclusive business models: IFAD case studies' [pdf] <https://www.ifad.org/documents/10180/9f4878e8-6353-4aa8-8c76-5b03938c641c> [accessed 7 October 2016].

IFAD (n. d. c) 'Peru: Puno Cusco Corridor Development Project' [pdf] <http://operations.ifad.org/documents/654016/72ba5d7c-7595-4540-9afd-b2d401e8d0b3> [accessed 7 October 2016].

IFAD, Environment and Climate Division (2015) *The Policy Advantage: Enabling Smallholders' Adaptation Priorities to be Realized* [online]. IFAD, Rome. Available from: https://www.

ifad.org/documents/10180/16492d6f-f842-4695-9493-4e5fbdd1c6af [accessed 7 October 2016].

IFAD, Financing Facility for Remittances (2013) *Remittances and Mobile Banking* [online]. IFAD, Rome. Available from https://www.ifad.org/documents/10180/651e18a5-0d3b-46a0-985f-d87ffb2eab0e [accessed 10 October 2016].

IFAD, India Country Office (2011) *Trail Blazers: Lighting the Way Ahead* [online]. IFAD India Country Office, New Delhi. Available from: https://www.ifad.org/documents/10180/6566a2a2-0b9f-41cd-9fe4-6f43c22ffde9 [accessed 7 October 2016].

IFAD, Near East, North Africa and Europe Division, Programme Management Department (2013) *Al Dhala Community Resource Management Project Supervision report: Main report and appendices*, 3285-YE [online]. IFAD, Rome. Available from: <http://operations.ifad.org/documents/654016/5bc212e0-8643-4dda-91c8-4c1aedbd7674> [accessed 6 October 2016].

IFAD, Policy and Technical Advisory Division (2016) *Lessons Learned: Digital Financial Services for Smallholder Households*, Lessons Learned [online]. IFAD, Rome. Available from: https://www.ifad.org/documents/10180/26e590e3-1398-433a-9586-5c27d7bee04d [accessed 7 October 2016].

IFAD, Policy and Technical Advisory Division (2016) *Lessons Learned: Reducing Women's Domestic Workload Through Water Investments*, Lessons Learned [online]. IFAD, Rome. Available from: https://www.ifad.org/documents/10180/412e2759-c0b9-4451-99f5-6c72b4af84e6 [accessed 7 October 2016].

IFAD, Programme Management Department (2013) 'IFAD's performance in fragile states' [pdf] <https://www.ifad.org/documents/10180/5336d6b5-297f-4e03-89d0-1ff79131629f> [accessed 6 October 2016].

IFAD, West and Central Africa Division, Programme Management Department (2014) 'Project for the Promotion of Local Initiative for Development in Aguié: Project Completion Report Digest', Project No. 1221 [pdf] <http://operations.ifad.org/documents/654016/26904d60-316a-4a2d-84ac-a88dbacdc063> [accessed 10 October 2016].

IFAD Governing Council (2013) 'Thirty-sixth Session Report: Rome 13-14 February 2013', GC 36 [pdf] <https://webapps.ifad.org/members/gc/36/docs/GC-36-Report.pdf> [accessed 10 October 2016].

IFAD Newsroom (2013) 'Queen Maxima and Senior UN Officials visit Ethiopia and Tanzania to highlight the role of financial inclusion in improving the lives of rural poor' [website] <https://www.ifad.org/en/newsroom/press_release/past/tags/m13/y2013/2598977> (posted 9 December 2013) [accessed 7 October 2016].

IFAD Newsroom (2014) 'Smallholder farmers are more than climate victims – says IFAD report' [website] <https://www.ifad.org/en/newsroom/press_release/tags/p78/y2014/6860725> (posted 3 December 2014) [accessed 10 October 2016].

IFAD Newsroom (2015) 'Remittances from Europe top US$109 billion, providing lifeline to millions worldwide' [website] <https://www.ifad.org/en/newsroom/press_release/tags/p46/y2015/7675550> [accessed 10 October 2016].

IFAD Operations (n.d. a) 'Agropastoral Value Chains Project in the Governorate of Médenine' [website] <http://operations.ifad.org/web/ifad/operations/country/project/tags/tunisia/1704/project_overview> [accessed 8 September 2016].

IFAD Operations (n.d. b) 'Community-Based Natural Resource Management Programme – Niger Delta' [website]

<http://operations.ifad.org/web/ifad/operations/country/project/tags/nigeria/1260/project_overview> [accessed 15 September 2016].

IFAD Operations (n.d. c) 'IFAD's strategy in Burundi' [website] <http://operations.ifad.org/web/ifad/operations/country/home/tags/burundi > [accessed 8 September 2016].

IFAD Operations (n.d. d) 'Rural Finance Institution-Building Programme (RUFIN)' [website] <http://operations.ifad.org/web/ifad/operations/country/project/tags/nigeria/1212/project_overview> [accessed 8 September 2016].

IFAD Operations (n.d. e) 'Vocational Training and Agricultural Productivity Improvement Programme (FORMAPROD)' [website] <http://operations.ifad.org/web/ifad/operations/country/project/tags/madagascar/1516/project_overview> [accessed 24 August 2016].

IFAD Operations (n.d. f) 'West Noubaria Rural Development Project' [website] <http://operations.ifad.org/web/ifad/operations/country/project/tags/egypt/1204/project_overview> [accessed 8 September 2016].

IFAD Stories (2016a) 'Building a successful business in China' [website] <https://www.ifad.org/stories/tags/china/26771920> (posted 4 July 2016) [accessed 7 October 2016].

IFAD Stories (2016b) 'Why are rural youth leaving farming?' [website] <https://www.ifad.org/stories/tags/senegal/17593915> (posted 6 April 2016) [accessed 7 October 2016].

IFADTV (2012) *Brazil: Grey Water, Green Ground* [video] <https://www.youtube.com/watch?v=mq-p8Bf2880> (posted 22 May 2012) [accessed 10 October 2016].

IFADTV (2013) *Bolivia: Crazy for Quinoa* [video] <https://www.youtube.com/watch?v=z4oZtVmWgOw> (posted 13 February 2013) [accessed 7 October 2016].

IFADTV (2014) *Cambodia: The Software Solution* [video] <https://www.youtube.com/watch?v=DBOCGSzEidk> (posted 18 September 2014) [accessed 10 October 2016].

IFADTV (2016a) *Aleem Ahmed: Teff Talk* [video]<https://www.youtube.com/watch?v=vNvXpLIhuME> (posted 16 May 2016) [accessed 7 October 2016].

IFADTV (2016b) *Laos: Nutritious Entertainment* [video] <https://www.youtube.com/watch?v=fmfsE31-yCA> (posted 3 March 2016) [accessed 10 October 2016].

IFPRI (2016) *Global Nutrition Report 2016: From Promise to Impact: Ending Malnutrition by 2030* [online]. IFPRI, Washington, DC. Available from: http://ebrary.ifpri.org/utils/getfile/collection/p15738coll2/id/130354/filename/130565.pdf [accessed 10 October 2016].

Inter-Agency Standing Committee (IASC) (2015) 'Humanitarian crisis in Yemen: Gender alert July 2015' [online]. IASC, Geneva. Available from: http://www2.unwomen.org/~/media/headquarters/attachments/sections/news/stories/2015/iasc%20gender%20reference%20group%20-%20yemen%20gender%20alert%20july%202015.pdf?v=1&d=20150731T154037 [accessed 7 October 2016].

IOM (2016) 'Mediterranean migrant arrivals in 2016 pass 76,000; Deaths top 400' [website] <http://www.iom.int/news/mediterranean-migrant-arrivals-2016-pass-76000-deaths-top-400> (posted 9 February 2016) [accessed 6 October 2016].

IRRI (n.d. a) 'Climate change-ready rice' [website] <http://irri.org/our-work/research/better-rice-varieties/climate-change-ready-rice> [accessed 15 August 2016].

IRRI (n.d. b) 'Science of C4 Rice' [website]<http://c4rice.irri.org/index.php/19-about/57-science-of-c4-rice> [accessed 9 September 2016].

ITU (2014) 'ITU releases 2014 ICT figures' [website] <http://www.itu.int/net/pressoffice/press_releases/2014/23.aspx#.V9kW7fl96Uk> (posted 5 May 2014) [accessed 10 October 2016].

Kaminski, J. and Christiaensen, L. (2014) 'Post-harvest loss in Sub-Saharan Africa: What do farmers say?' Policy Research Working Paper 6831 [online]. World Bank, Washington, DC. Available from: http://documents.worldbank.org/curated/en/782981468008454485/pdf/WPS6831.pdf [accessed 7 October 2016].

Kar, D. and Spanjers, J. (2015) *Illicit Financial Flows from Developing Countries: 2004-2013* [online]. Global Financial Integrity, Washington, DC. Available from: http://www.gfintegrity.org/wp-content/uploads/2015/12/IFF-Update_2015-Final.pdf [accessed 6 October 2016].

Kelley, C.P., Mohtadi, S., Cane, M.A., Seager, R. and Kushnir, Y. (2015) 'Climate change in the Fertile Crescent and implications of the recent Syrian drought', *Proceedings of the National Academy of Sciences* 112(11), pp. 3241–46.

Kharas, H. (2010) 'The emerging middle class in developing countries,' OECD Development Centre Working Paper No. 285 [online]. Available from: https://www.oecd.org/dev/44457738.pdf [accessed 6 October 2016].

Koo, J. (2013) 'Minding the yield gap in Africa: A country-level analysis,' [website], HarvestChoice, <https://harvestchoice.org/labs/minding-yield-gap-africa-country-level-analysis> (posted 23 May 2013) [accessed 7 October 2016].

Ledwith, T. (2012) 'Sweet success: Revitalizing cocoa production and export in São Tome and Principe'[blog] IFAD Social Reporting Blog <http://ifad-un.blogspot.ca/2012/12/sweet-success-revitalizing-cocoa.html> (posted 13 December 2012) [accessed 7 October 2016].

Leke, A., Lund, S., Roxburgh, C. and van Wamelen, A. (2010) 'What's driving Africa's growth' [website], McKinsey & Company <http://www.mckinsey.com/global-themes/middle-east-and-africa/whats-driving-africas-growth> (posted June 2010) [accessed 10 October 2016].

Lerman, Z. and Sutton, W.R. (2006) 'Productivity and efficiency of small and large farms in Moldova', paper presented at the American Agricultural Economics Association Annual Meeting, Long Beach, CA, 23–26 July 2006 [online]. Available from: <http://ageconsearch.umn.edu/bitstream/21085/1/sp06le03.pdf> [accessed 6 October 2016].

Livingston, G., Schonberger, S. and Delaney, S. (2011) 'Sub-Saharan Africa: The state of smallholders in agriculture', paper presented at Conference on New Directions for Smallholder Agriculture, IFAD, Rome, 24–25 January 2011 [online]. Available from: <https://www.ifad.org/documents/10180/78d97354-8d30-466e-b75c-9406bf47779c> [accessed 7 October 2016].

Making Sense (n.d.) 'Rural Youth Economic Empowerment Program 2013–16' [website] <http://www.makingcents.com/makingcentsprojects/if46fbwq58/Rural-Youth-Economic-Empowerment-Program> [accessed 8 September 2016].

Mattern, M. and Tarazi, M. (2015) *Designing Digital Financial Services for Smallholder Families: Lessons from Zimbabwe, Senegal, Rwanda, and Cambodia*, Perspectives 1 [online]. CGAP, Washington, DC. Available from: <https://www.cgap.org/sites/default/files/Perspectives-Designing-Digital-Financial-Services-for-Smallholder-Families-Oct-2015.pdf> [accessed 7 October 2016].

Munang, R. and Mgendi, R. (2015) 'Is the Africa Rising cliché sustainable? Toward environmentally sustainable and socially inclusive growth in Africa. *Environment: Science and Policy for Sustainable Development*, 57(3), pp. 4–18 <http://dx.doi.org/10.1080/00139157.2015.1025641>.

NEPAD (2003) *Comprehensive Africa Agriculture Development Programme* [online]. NEPAD, Midrand. Available from: <http://www.nepad-caadp.net/download/file/fid/591> [accessed 10 October 2016].

Norgaard, R.B. (1988) 'The biological control of cassava mealybug in Africa', *American Journal of Agricultural Economics*, 70(2), pp. 366–71 <http://dx.doi.org/10.2307/1242077>.

Nwanze, K.F. (2012a) 'Growing peace through development', Viewpoint 3 [online]. IFAD, Rome. Available from: <https://www.ifad.org/documents/10180/0bccd7e4-a171-4e72-b75e-2aa2bfd91f93> [accessed 6 October 2016].

Nwanze, K.F. (2012b) 'Reaching food security means reaching out to smallholders' [blog] IFAD Social Reporting Blog. <http://ifad-un.blogspot.it/2012/05/reaching-food-security-means-reaching.html> (posted 14 May 2012) [accessed 7 October 2016].

Nwanze, K.F. (2014) 'A healthy, peaceful and secure Africa is now within our grasp', *The Guardian* [website] <https://www.theguardian.com/global-development/poverty-matters/2014/jun/20/kanayo-nwanze-africa-leaders-deliver-promises> (posted 20 June 2014) [accessed 10 October 2016].

OECD (2016) 'Development aid rises again in 2015, spending on refugees doubles' [website] <http://www.oecd.org/dac/development-aid-rises-again-in-2015-spending-on-refugees-doubles.htm> (posted 13 April 2016) [accessed 6 October 2016].

ONE (2013) 'The Maputo Commitments and the 2014 African Union Year of Agriculture' [pdf] <https://s3.amazonaws.com/one.org/images/131008_ONE_Maputo_FINAL.pdf> (posted 9 October 2013) [accessed 10 October 2016].

Opportunity International (n.d.) *Financing Smallholder Farmers to Increase Incomes and Transform Lives in Rural Communities* [online]. Opportunity International: Oak Brook. Available from: <https://opportunity.org/content/News/Publications/Knowledge%20Exchange/Financing-Smallholder-Farmers-Opportunity-International.pdf> [accessed 10 October 2016].

Oteng, J.W. and Sant'Anna, R. (1999) 'Rice production in Africa: current situation and issues', in Tran, D.V. (ed.) *International Rice Commission Newsletter*, vol. 48 [online]. FAO, Rome. Available from: http://www.fao.org/docrep/003/x2243t/x2243t00.htm#TopOfPage [accessed 10 October 2016].

Page, J. (2014) 'Africa's failure to industrialize: Bad luck or bad policy?' [blog], Brookings, <https://www.brookings.edu/blog/africa-in-focus/2014/11/20/africas-failure-to-industrialize-bad-luck-or-bad-policy/> (posted 20 November 2014) [accessed 7 October 2016].

Papademetriou, M.K. (2000) 'Rice production in the Asia-Pacific region: Issues and perspectives', in Papademetriou, M.K., Dent, F.J. and Herath, E.M. (eds) *Bridging the Rice Yield Gap in the Asia-Pacific Region* [online]. FAO Regional Office for Asia and the Pacific, Bangkok. Available from: http://www.fao.org/docrep/003/x6905e/x6905e00.htm#Contents [accessed 10 October 2016].

Paqui, D. (2011) 'IFAD supported South Gansu Poverty Reduction Programme is challenging the 2000 Millennium Summit' [blog], IFAD Social Reporting Blog <http://ifad-un.blogspot.it/2011/08/ifad-supported-south-gansu-poverty.html> (posted 5 August 2011) [accessed 10 October 2016].

Platform for Agricultural Risk Management (n.d.) 'Who we are' [website] <http://p4arm.org/who-we-are/> [accessed 8 September 2016].

Reij, C. (2009) 'Regreening the Sahel: The success of natural tree regeneration', *Farming Matters* [website] <http://www.agriculturesnetwork.org/magazines/global/scaling-

up-and-sustaining-the-gains/regreening-the-sahel-the-success-of-natural-tree> (posted December 2009) [accessed 10 October 2016].

Reij, C. (2012) 'Update no. 2: Impressions of Niger in January 2012' [blog] Africa Regreening Initiatives <http://africa-regreening.blogspot.it/2012/01/update-no-2-impressions-of-niger-in.html> (posted 25 January 2012) [accessed 10 October 2016].

Reinke, E. and Sperandini, S. (2012) 'M-PESA: The power of mobile technology in livestock marketing. Kenya Learning Route, case 3' [blog], IFAD Social Reporting Blog <http://ifad-un.blogspot.it/2012/03/m-pesa-power-of-mobile-technology-in.html> (posted 4 March 2012) [accessed 7 October 2016].

Remittances Gateway (2014) 'Leader of Branchless Banking: Easypaisa Makes Transaction of Rs 178 Billion in 3-Year' [website] <http://www.remittancesgateway.org/leader-of-branchless-banking-easypaisa-makes-transaction-of-rs-178-billion-in-3-year/> [accessed 10 October 2016].

RIMISP (2016) *Poverty and Inequality: Latin America Report* [online]. RIMISP, Santiago. Available from: http://reliefweb.int/sites/reliefweb.int/files/resources/Sintesis-Rimisp-Ing-2015-V4-Completo.pdf [accessed 7 October 2016].

Riquet, C. (2013) 'Small farmers, mobile banking, financial inclusion in Madagascar' [blog], CGAP, <http://www.cgap.org/blog/small-farmers-mobile-banking-financial-inclusion-madagascar> (posted 28 October 2013) [accessed 7 October 2016].

Rural Poverty Portal (2012) 'In Ethiopia and six other nations, UN agencies join hands to empower poor rural women' [website] <http://www.ruralpovertyportal.org/country/voice/tags/ethiopia/ethiopia_women> [accessed 7 October 2016].

Rural Poverty Portal (2013) 'Women, unity, water: Adapting to climate change and improving livelihoods in Swaziland' [website] <http://www.ruralpovertyportal.org/country/voice/

tags/swaziland/swaziland_climate> (posted 15 May 2013) [accessed 7 October 2016].

Rural Poverty Portal (n.d. a) 'Boosting knowledge and financial security in Peru' [website] <http://www.ruralpovertyportal.org/country/voice/tags/peru/peru_financial#> [accessed 9 September 2016].

Rural Poverty Portal (n.d. b) 'China biogas project turns waste into energy' [website] <http://www.ruralpovertyportal.org/country/voice/tags/china/biogas> [accessed 15 August 2016].

Rural Poverty Portal (n.d. c) 'Drip irrigation technology in Madagascar: a successful example of scaling up' [website] <http://www.ruralpovertyportal.org/country/voice/tags/madagascar/madagascar_scampis> [accessed 15 September 2016].

Rural Poverty Portal (n.d. d) 'Growing rural businesses in the Republic of Moldova' [website] <http://www.ruralpovertyportal.org/country/voice/tags/moldova/moldova_growing> [accessed 15 September 2016].

Rural Poverty Portal (n.d. e) 'La pauvreté rurale au Bénin' [website] <http://www.ruralpovertyportal.org/country/home/tags/benin> [accessed 24 August 2016].

Rural Poverty Portal (n.d. f) 'Organic and fair trade production revitalize cocoa industry in São Tome and Principe' [website] <http://www.ruralpovertyportal.org/en/region/voice/tags/africa/saotome_voice> [accessed 15 September 2016].

Rural Poverty Portal (n.d. g) 'Organic Moldovan "Queen" scoops international cheese prize' [website] <http://www.ruralpovertyportal.org/country/voice/tags/moldova/moldova_prize> [accessed 15 September 2016].

Rural Poverty Portal (n.d. h) 'Organics: The key to helping Pacific agriculture conquer new markets' [website] <http://www.ruralpovertyportal.org/en/region/voice/tags/oceania/organics_pacific> [accessed 15 September 2016].

Rural Poverty Portal (n.d. i) 'Rural poverty in Moldova' [website] <http://www.ruralpovertyportal.org/country/home/tags/moldova> [accessed 15 September 2016].

Rural Poverty Portal (n.d. j) 'Strategic partnerships breathe life and hope into an impoverished community in Brazil' [website] <http://www.ruralpovertyportal.org/country/voice/tags/brazil/camara> [accessed 24 August 2016].

Rural Poverty Portal (n.d. k) 'Wheelbarrows, a road and a future: South Pacific islanders rediscover their power to change their lives' [website] <http://www.ruralpovertyportal.org/country/voice/tags/tonga/mordi_tonga> [accessed 15 September 2016].

Save the Children, *A Wake-Up Call: Lesson from Ebola for the World's Health Systems* [online]. Save the Children, London. Available from: http://www.savethechildren.org/atf/cf/%7B9def2ebe-10ae-432c-9bd0-df91d2eba74a%7D/WAKE%20UP%20CALL%20REPORT%20PDF.PDF [accessed 10 October 2016].

Slavchevska, V., Kaaria, S. and Taivalmaa, S. (2016) 'Feminization of agriculture in the context of rural transformations: What is the evidence?' Working paper [online]. World Bank, Washington, DC. Available from: http://documents.worldbank.org/curated/en/127411474615736032/pdf/108468-WP-P159499-PUBLIC-ABSTRACT-SENT-WorkingPaperFeminizationofAgricultureWorldBankFAO.pdf [accessed 7 October 2016].

Sooretul (n.d.) 'Le concept de sooretul, qu'est-ce-donc?' [website] Sooretul, <http://www.sooretul.com/account/about-us/> [accessed 15 September 2016].

Tacoli, C. (2015) 'Creating a new menu for food security policy', International Institute for Environment and Development Briefing [online]. Available from: http://pubs.iied.org/17331IIED.html [accessed 7 October 2016].

Thapa, G. (2009) 'Smallholder farming in transforming economies of Asia and the Pacific: Challenges and opportunities', Discussion Paper prepared for the side event organized during the thirty-third session of IFAD's Governing Council, 18 February 2009 [online]. Available from: https://www.ifad.org/documents/10180/a194177c-54b7-43d0-a82e-9bad64b76e82 [accessed 6 October 2016].

Tole, B. (2014) 'Nairobi Sharefair calls for enhanced access to technologies that are sensitive to rural women's aspirations', [blog] IFAD Social Reporting Blog <http://ifad-un.blogspot.it/2014/10/nairobi-sharefair-calls-for-enhanced.html> (posted 24 October 2014)[accessed 3 November 2016].

UN (2010) 'Goal 7: Ensure environmental Sustainability' DPI/2650 G [pdf] <http://www.un.org/millenniumgoals/pdf/MDG_FS_7_EN.pdf> [accessed 10 October 2016].

UN (2014) *Agriculture: Global Alliance for Climate-Smart Agriculture, Action Plan* [pdf] <http://www.un.org/climatechange/summit/wp-content/uploads/sites/2/2014/09/AGRICULTURE-Action-Plan.pdf> [accessed 7 October 2016].

UN (2015) *The Millennium Development Goals Report 2015* [pdf] <http://www.un.org/millenniumgoals/2015_MDG_Report/pdf/MDG%202015%20rev%20(July%201).pdf> [accessed 6 October 2016].

UN Department of Economic and Social Affairs (UN/DESA) (2015) *The World's Women 2015: Trends and Statistics* [online]. UN/DESA, New York, NY. Available from: http://unstats.un.org/unsd/gender/downloads/WorldsWomen2015_report.pdf [accessed 3 November 2016].

UN Department of Economic and Social Affairs, Population Division (2015) *World Population Prospects: The 2015 Revision*, Vol. I: Comprehensive Tables (ST/ESA/SER.A/379) [online]. Available from: https://esa.un.org/unpd/wpp/Publications/Files/WPP2015_Volume-I_Comprehensive-Tables.pdf [accessed 6 October 2016].

UN Economic and Social Council (2014) 'Ebola epidemic could drain US$3-4 billion from Sub-Saharan African economy, reverse peacebuilding gains in hardest-hit nations, Economic and Social Council told', 2015 session, 3rd meeting, ECOSOC/6653 [website] <http://www.un.org/press/en/2014/ecosoc6653.doc.htm> (posted 5 December 2014) [accessed 10 October 2016].

UN Environment Management Group (UNEMG) (2011) *Global Drylands: A UN System-Wide Response* [online]. UNEMG, Geneva. Available from: http://www.unccd.int/Lists/SiteDocumentLibrary/Publications/Global_Drylands_Full_Report.pdf [accessed 7 October 2016].

UNESCO Institute for Statistics (2016) '50th anniversary of international literacy day: Literacy rates are on the rise but millions remain illiterate', UIS Fact Sheet No. 38 [pdf]. <http://www.uis.unesco.org/literacy/Documents/fs38-literacy-en.pdf> [accessed 21 November 2016].

UN Framework Convention on Climate Change (UNFCCC) (2015) 'Paris Agreement' [pdf] <https://unfccc.int/files/meetings/paris_nov_2015/application/pdf/paris_agreement_english_.pdf> [accessed 7 October 2016].

UN General Assembly (2015a) *Addis Ababa Action Agenda of the Third International Conference on Financing for Development (Addis Ababa Action Agenda)* (17 August 2015, Resolution 69/313) [online]. Available from http://undocs.org/A/RES/69/313 [accessed 7 October 2016].

UN General Assembly (2015b) *Transforming our World: The 2030 Agenda for Sustainable Development* (25 September 2015, A/RES/70/1) [online]. Available from: http://undocs.org/A/RES/70/1 [accessed 6 October 2016].

UN-Habitat (2006) *State of the World's Cities 2006/7* [online]. Earthscan, Sterling. Available from: http://unhabitat.org/books/state-of-the-worlds-cities-20062007/ [accessed 7 October 2016].

UN-Habitat (2007) *Global Report on Human Settlements 2007: Enhancing Urban Safety and Security* [online]. UN-Habitat, Nairobi. Available from: http://unhabitat.org/books/global-report-on-human-settlements-2007-enhancing-urban-safety-and-security/ [accessed 7 October 2016].

UNICEF (2013) *Improving Child Nutrition: The Achievable Imperative for Global Progress* [online]. UNICEF, New York, NY. Available from: http://www.unicef.org/publications/files/Nutrition_Report_final_lo_res_8_April.pdf [accessed 10 October 2016].

UNICEF (n.d.) 'Goal: Promote gender equality and empower women' [website] <http://www.unicef.org/mdg/index_genderequality.htm> [accessed 9 September 2016].

United Nations Intergovernmental Committee of Experts on Sustainable Development Financing (2014) *Report of the Intergovernmental Committee of Experts on Sustainable Development Financing* [online]. UN, New York, NY. Available from http://www.un.org/esa/ffd/wp-content/uploads/2014/12/ICESDF.pdf [accessed 10 October 2016].

UN Population Fund (UNFPA) (2014) *The State of the World Population 2014: The Power of 1.8 Billion Adolescents, Youth and the Transformation of the Future* [online]. UNFPA, New York. Available from: https://www.unfpa.org/sites/default/files/pub-pdf/EN-SWOP14-Report_FINAL-web.pdf [accessed 7 October 2016].

UNSGSA (2013) 'Giving a boost to agriculture through inclusive finance in Ethiopia' [website] <https://www.unsgsa.org/resources/country-visits/giving-boost-agriculture-through-inclusive-finance-ethiopia/> (posted 11 December 2013) [accessed 10 October 2016].

UNTT Working Group on Sustainable Development Financing (2013) 'Financing for sustainable development: Review of global investment requirement estimates,' Chapter 1 [pdf]

<https://sustainabledevelopment.un.org/content/documents/2096Chapter%201-global%20investment%20requirement%20estimates.pdf> [accessed 10 October 2016].

UN Women (2015) Progress of the World's Women 2015–2016: Transforming Economies, Realizing Rights. <http://progress.unwomen.org/en/2015/>

USAID (2016) 'Food assistance fact sheet – Burundi' [website] <https://www.usaid.gov/burundi/food-assistance> (last modified 3 June 2016) [accessed 6 October 2016].

U.S. Geological Survey (USGS) (2016) *Mineral Commodity Summaries 2016* [online]. USGS, Washington, DC. <http://dx.doi.org/10.3133/70140094>.

Varshney, R.K., Chen, W., Li, Y., Bharti, A.K., Saxena, R.K., Schlueter, J.A., Donoghue, M.T., Azam, S., Fan, G., Whaley, A.M. and Farmer, A.D. (2012) 'Draft genome sequence of pigeonpea (Cajanus cajan), an orphan legume crop of resource-poor farmers', *Nature biotechnology*, 30(1), pp. 83–89 <http://dx.doi.org/10.1038/nbt.2022>.

Virmani, P. (2014) 'Note to India's leaders: your 150m young people are calling for change', *The Guardian* [website] <https://www.theguardian.com/commentisfree/2014/apr/08/india-leaders-young-people-change-2014-elections> (posted 8 April 2014) [accessed 7 October 2016].

von Kaenel, C. (2015) 'Farms harvest cuts in carbon dioxide via soil: Farming to improve crops and store more CO2 gains traction', *Scientific American*, Climate Wire [website] <http://www.scientificamerican.com/article/farms-harvest-cuts-in-carbon-dioxide-via-soil/> (posted 22 September 2015) [accessed 7 October 2016].

Walker, T., with Hash, T., Rattunde, F. and Weltzien, E. (2016) *Improved Crop Productivity for Africa's Drylands* [online].

World Bank Studies, Washington, DC. <http://dx.doi.org/10.1596/978-1-4648-0896-8> [accessed 7 October 2016].

WHO (2016) 'Ebola data and Statistics' [website] <http://apps.who.int/gho/data/view.ebola-sitrep.ebola-summary-latest?lang=en> (posted 11 May 2016) [accessed 10 October 2016].

WHO/UNICEF Joint Monitoring Programme (2015) *Progress on Sanitation and Drinking Water, 2015 Update and MDG Assessment* [online]. WHO, Geneva. Available from: http://www.wssinfo.org/fileadmin/user_upload/resources/JMP-Update-report-2015_English.pdf [accessed 7 October 2016].

Woetzel, J., Madgavkar, A., Ellingrud, K., Labaye, E., Devillard, S., Kutcher, E., Manyika, J., Dobbs, R. and Krishnan, M. (2015) 'The power of parity: How advancing women's equality can add US$12 trillion to global growth', McKinsey Global Institute [website] <http://www.mckinsey.com/global-themes/employment-and-growth/how-advancing-womens-equality-can-add-12-trillion-to-global-growth> [accessed 7 October 2016].

World Bank (2009) *World Development Report 2009: Reshaping Economic Geography* [online]. World Bank, Washington, DC. Available from: http://siteresources.worldbank.org/INTWDRS/Resources/477365-1327525347307/8392086-1327528510568/WDR09_bookweb_2.pdf [accessed 10 October 2016].

World Bank (2012) *World Development Report 2012: Gender Equality and Development* [online]. World Bank, Washington, DC. Available from: http://hdl.handle.net/10986/4391 [accessed 7 October 2016].

World Bank (2013) *Financing for Development Post-2015* [pdf] <http://documents.worldbank.org/curated/en/206701468158366611/Financing-for-development-post-2015> [accessed 6 October 2016].

World Bank (2015) *Remittance Prices Worldwide*, no. 16 [pdf] <https://remittanceprices.worldbank.org/sites/default/files/rpw_report_december_2015.pdf> [accessed 10 October 2016].

World Bank (n.d. a) 'Fertilizer consumption (kilograms per hectare of arable land)' [website] <http://data.worldbank.org/indicator/AG.CON.FERT.ZS?locations=ZG> [accessed 28 September 2016].

World Bank (n.d. b) 'Harmonized list of fragile situations FY14' [website] <http://siteresources.worldbank.org/EXTLICUS/Resources/511777-1269623894864/HarmonizedlistoffragilestatesFY14.pdf> [accessed 29 September 2016].

World Bank (n.d. c) 'Sub-Saharan Africa' [website] <http://povertydata.worldbank.org/poverty/region/SSA> [accessed 29 September 2016].

World Bank (n.d. d) 'World Bank country and lending groups' [website] <https://datahelpdesk.worldbank.org/knowledgebase/articles/906519> [accessed 28 September 2016].

World Bank, Migration and Remittances Team, Development Prospects Group (2015) 'Migration and remittances: Recent developments and outlook, special topic: Financing for development,' Migration and Development Brief 24 [pdf] <https://siteresources.worldbank.org/INTPROSPECTS/Resources/334934-1288990760745/MigrationandDevelopmentBrief24.pdf> (posted 13 April 2015) [accessed 6 October 2016].

World Cocoa Foundation (2014) *Cocoa Market Update* [online]. World Cocoa Foundation, Washington, DC. Available from: http://www.worldcocoafoundation.org/wp-content/uploads/Cocoa-Market-Update-as-of-4-1-2014.pdf [accessed 7 October 2016].

World Food Conference General Assembly (1974), *Universal Declaration on the Eradication of Hunger and Malnutrition* (16 November 1974, Resolution 3180) [online]. Available from: http://www.ohchr.org/EN/ProfessionalInterest/Pages/EradicationOfHungerAndMalnutrition.aspx [accessed 28 September 2016].

World Food Prize (n.d. a) '2004: Jones and Yuan' [website] <http://www.worldfoodprize.org/en/laureates/20002009_laureates/2004_jones_and_yuan/> [accessed 29 September 2016].

World Food Prize (n.d. b) '1995: Herren' [website] <http://www.worldfoodprize.org/en/laureates/19871999_laureates/1995_herren/> [accessed 29 September 2016].

You, L., Ringler, C., Wood-Sichra, U., Robertson, R., Wood, S., Zhu, T., Nelson, G., Guo, Z. and Sun, Y. (2011) 'What is the irrigation potential for Africa? A combined biophysical and socioeconomic approach', *Food Policy*, 36(6), pp. 770–82 <http://dx.doi.org/10.1016/j.foodpol.2011.09.001>.